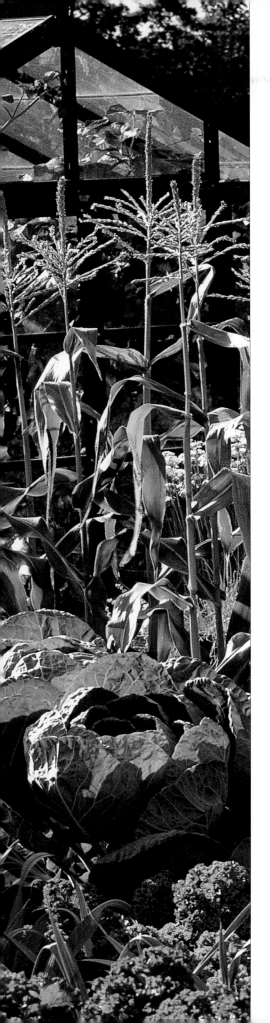

GROWING FRUIT AND VEGETABLES

A practical guide to fruit and vegetable growing

RICHARD BIRD

LORENZ BOOKS

First published in 2001 by Lorenz Books

© Anness Publishing Limited 2001

Lorenz Books is an imprint of
Anness Publishing Limited
Hermes House
88–89 Blackfriars Road
London SE1 8HA

Published in the USA by Lorenz Books
Anness Publishing Inc.
27 West 20th Street, New York, NY 10011

Distributed in Canada by Raincoast Books, 8680 Cambie Street, Vancouver
British Columbia V6P 6M9

Publisher: Joanna Lorenz
Senior Editor: Caroline Davison
Project Editor: Emma Hardy
Designer: Ruth Hope
Production Controller: Steve Lang
Illustrator: Liz Pepperell

Previously published as part of a larger compendium, *The Kitchen Garden Book*

1 3 5 7 9 10 8 6 4 2

Publishers' note: In the United States, the
burning of plants or bulbs (if they are diseased,
for example) is prohibited.

introduction

ABOVE **This is a traditional kitchen garden, with vegetables neatly lined up in rows. Although it is autumn, there will be plenty of vegetables in season over the next few months.**

BELOW **Raised beds create a greater depth of fertile soil, so the vegetables can be planted much closer together.**

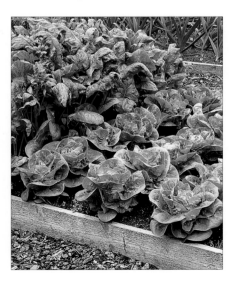

At a time when a seemingly limitless range of produce is available in supermarkets, it may seem odd that so many people are still choosing to grow their own fruit and vegetables, but there are a number of good reasons for this. For some people, a major factor is saving money, but for many others, the pleasure of getting close to the soil, listening to the birds and breathing the scents of nature is far more important.

The quality of home grown fruit and vegetables is far superior to anything that you are likely to find in the shops. To begin with, they are fresh - literally in the ground one minute and in the pot the next! If you only need one stalk of celery, you can just cut one stalk, leaving the rest in the ground to stay fresh for the next time you need it. So you can always be sure that both flavour and nutritional value are at their peak.

Secondly, there is a huge choice of varieties available to gardeners, most of them bred with taste as the main consideration, as well as resistance to pests and diseases. Commercial growers, however, have quite different priorities, they want to grow produce that will arrive at the shops looking fresh and undamaged, and so the produce has tough skins, which also gives them a long shelf life. Taste, if it plays a part at all, is often at the bottom of the list. Gardeners, however, put a much greater value on taste and will select varieties with this firmly in mind, regardless of the

vegetable's optimum size or the fact that it may be

irregular in shape. And, the shelf life of produce is

irrelevant when you can pick it fresh as you need it and

bring it straight to the kitchen.

A further consideration, increasingly important for

may people, is concern about the large quantities of

chemicals used by commercial growers. Today, gardeners

choose to use few chemical sprays and powders, but

crops bought from the supermarkets have been doused

in an ever-increasing number of compounds to ensure

that, among other things, they come to the shops in a

totally umblemished state.

ABOVE **With the addition of flowers, this vegetable garden is not only productive, but also decorative.**

Finally, as well as having healthy food, perhaps what

the gardener benefits from the most is exercise and fresh air. There is also a

sense of closeness to nature, a cliché, perhaps, but there is still something

fundamental about getting your hands dirty and listening to the birds as you

work. Whether you are a seasoned grower, or just trying it for the first time,

with a large allotment or just a dwarf fruit tree or a few lettuces in the flower

beds, you will soon acquire a whole set of skills, many of them handed down

over the centuries, and of course, the very real satisfaction of growing your

own produce.

vegetables

Vegetables are the mainstay of any kitchen garden. The quantities and varieties as well as the way in which the crops are laid out will be determined by the preferences of the gardener. However, there are a few principles that apply to the growing of each type of vegetable, and these are described in this section of the book.

The gardener is spoilt for choice when it comes to the range of varieties available. At first it will be a question of experimenting to find the varieties whose taste you prefer as well as those that are best suited to the soil and climate in your garden. Once they have identified these varieties, many gardeners tend to stick with them. There is no harm in this, although it pays to be adventurous and to try not only a few new varieties, but also some types of vegetable that you have not grown before.

As well as buying seed, many gardeners collect their own. In this way they are certain to continue using the varieties that do well in their garden, especially if they collect seed from the best plants each time. F1 hybrids will not come true and it is not worth collecting seed from them, but it is worth experimenting with ordinary open-pollinated seed. Some plant seeds, like beans and peas, are easy to collect, but other plants, such as carrots, are biennial and do not set seed until the second year. Leaving plants in the ground for two years takes up valuable space and so it may not be worth it for these. Experiment, it will add to the fun of gardening, especially if you end up with your own strain of vegetables.

BULB VEGETABLES

Onions
Allium cepa

Onions are one of the oldest vegetables. They were grown by the Ancient Egyptians over 5,000 years ago and were probably eaten long before that. Their actual origins are not known, but they probably first grew in the mountainous regions of Central Asia. As well as adding flavour to food, they have long been known for their health-giving properties.

Traditionally, the large, round onions that are mainly used for cooking are grown from sets, which are small bulbs that have started their life during the previous season when they were sown as seed by seed merchants. They are harvested at the end of their first season, when they are approximately 1–2.5cm/ ½–1in in diameter. They are then either sold loose or, as is more frequently the case these days, they are pre-packaged and bought by weight or, less often, by number.

Some varieties can be grown from seed as long as they are sown early enough, and this usually means sowing under glass in midwinter in order to get a sufficiently long growing season. Another group, known as Japanese onions, has been developed for

sowing as seed or for planting out as sets in autumn for harvesting earlier than sets planted out in spring.

Smaller bulb onions are either shallots or pickling onions. Pickling onions are small, round onions that are grown from seed.

There are over one hundred different varieties of onion available. They can be broken down into three basic types according to colour: golden-brown, red and white. Most are round, but some varieties are torpedo-shaped. The main criteria – unless you are growing for showing, when uniformity and appearance are important – are taste and storage qualities. Golden varieties are generally best for storing, but the reds and whites provide, respectively, sweeter and milder flavours.

ABOVE **A good crop of onions growing in a block in a raised bed.**

Cultivation
Onions should be planted in an open position in a light soil that has been manured during the previous autumn. Plant the sets out in early spring.

Some varieties are heat treated, which prevents them from bolting, and they can be planted out later, in mid- to late spring when the soil is warmer. Plant them at 10cm/4in intervals in rows that are spaced about 30cm/12in apart. Plant with a dibber and cover the bulbs so that only the tips are showing.

Spring-sown seed can be sown in trays under glass in midwinter. Harden off and plant out in rows in mid-spring. Sow Japanese onions directly in beds in late summer or plant out as sets in early autumn.

Keep the plants weed free. There is generally no need to water unless the summer is particularly dry.

LEFT **The leaves of these onions are beginning to brown and have been moved to one side in order to speed up this process. This also allows maximum sunlight to reach the bulbs. Although not necessary, arranging the leaves in this way gives a satisfying beauty to a practical task.**

Cultivation

Sets
Planting time early spring (most varieties);
early summer (overwintering varieties)
Planting distance 10cm/4in
Distance between rows 25–30cm/10–12in
Harvesting late summer (most varieties);
midsummer (overwintering varieties)
Seed
Sowing time midwinter (under glass)
Sowing distance sow thinly
Sowing depth 1cm/½in
Distance between rows 25–30cm/10–12in
Thinning distance 5–10cm/2–4in
Harvesting late summer

RIGHT **Onions should be stored in trays in a frost-free shed.**

Harvesting

Onion bulbs can be lifted at any point in their growth for immediate use. However, for storage they must be fully developed, and the foliage should be beginning to die back. This is usually in late summer (midsummer for Japanese onions). As the foliage begins to turn yellow, lift each bulb slightly with a fork so that the roots start to break. Two weeks later carefully lift the bulbs. Clean off any soil and place them in a sunny, dry place to finish drying. A greenhouse is ideal, but if they are placed outside, move them under cover at night or if rain threatens.

Storage

Tie the onions into ropes or place them in net bags or on trays. Store them in a cool but frost-free place, such as a cellar, garage or shed. Check regularly, throwing out any that show signs of rotting.

Pests and diseases

The main pest is onion fly, whose maggots eat the onions, turning the leaves yellow and eventually killing them. Sets are less susceptible to onion fly than seed-grown onions are. Burn or destroy any affected bulbs. Onion eelworm produce distorted leaves. Again, burn or destroy affected plants.

Various fungal diseases, such as neck rot and white rot, can affect the bulbs. Destroy all infected bulbs.

Varieties

Bulb onion
'Ailsa Craig' spring- to late-summer-
sown seed, golden skinned
'Albion' spring-sown seed, white skinned
'Autumn Gold' sets, golden skinned
'Bedfordshire Champion' spring-sown
seed, golden skinned
'Buffalo' autumn-sown seed, golden skinned
'Dobie's All Rounder' sets, golden skinned
'Giant Fen Globe' sets, golden skinned
'Hygro' spring-sown seed,
golden skinned
'Mammoth Red' winter-sown
seed, red skinned
'Red Baron' sets, red skin and flesh
'Red Torpedo' late-summer
sown, red skinned
'Rocardo' sets, red skinned
'Sturon' sets,
golden skinned
'Stuttgart Giant' sets,
golden skinned
'White Prince' sets,
white skinned
Pickling onions
'Barletta'
'Giant Zittau'
'Paris Silver Skin'
'The Queen'

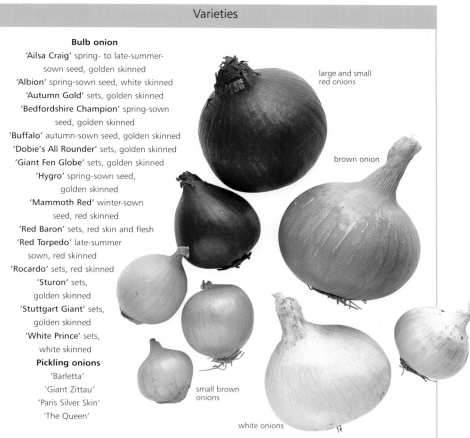

large and small red onions

brown onion

small brown onions

white onions

Shallots

Allium cepa Aggregatum Group

Shallots have been grown for almost as long as onions. They were originally named scallions after Ascalon (Ashqelon) in Israel, the place from where the Greeks thought the vegetable originated, but shallots probably originally came from Central Asia.

Shallots are widely used in cooking, especially in France, where small onions are preferred. Although they lack the strong smell of onions and do not make your eyes water, the taste is often more intense yet sweeter than that of onions, and they are used where delicate flavours are needed. The leaves are sometimes used as a substitute for chives, and in country areas shallots are often used as a substitute for pickling onions.

Shallots are a small form of onion, but instead of growing as single bulbs they tend to grow in bunches or clusters. The shapes and colours of shallots vary considerably, and France in particular has a great number of cultivars. Some are torpedo-shaped, others are rounded. The colour varies from yellows through browns to reds, and flavours range from delicate to strong.

Cultivation

An open, sunny position is required for growing shallots, and a light soil, which has been dug and manured during the previous autumn, is preferable. In the northern hemisphere the traditional day for planting shallots in many regions is

Plant the shallot bulbs in rows at 15–18cm/6–7in intervals with 30cm/12in between each row. Using a dibber or trowel, bury the bulbs so that only the tips are showing.

Boxing Day, but this is too early for most areas, and late winter or early spring is a better time. Set them out in rows, planting the individual bulbs at 15–18cm/6–7in intervals. Use a dibber or trowel, and bury the bulbs so that only the tips are showing. The rows should be 30cm/12in apart.

Keep weeded. Water in early summer if necessary.

Harvesting

When the foliage shrivels in midsummer, ease the shallots from the soil with a fork. Place them on staging in a greenhouse or on racks of wire netting to dry. Once the leaves have completely dried, remove any

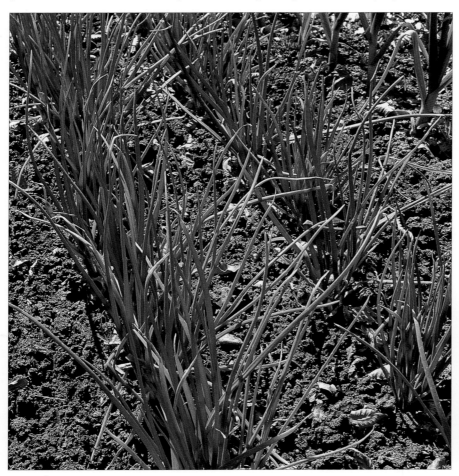

LEFT **Rows of shallots with garlic growing in the background.**

BELOW **Shallots drying on netting in the sunshine before being stored.**

dirt and dead foliage and break them up into individual bulbs before leaving to dry further.

Storage
Place shallots on wire racks or trays or in netting bags. Store them in a dark, cool but frost-free place, such as a cellar or garage. They should keep through the winter. Check on them regularly and throw out any that show signs of rotting.

Pests and diseases
On the whole, shallots are relatively trouble free, but they may succumb to the same

problems in terms of pests and diseases as onions. The main pest is likely to be onion eelworm, which produces distorted leaves. Onion fly may also be a problem. They lay their eggs in the bulbs, and the maggots then go on to eat the shallots, turning the leaves yellow and eventually killing them. Companion planting with parsley is a

ABOVE **A vigorous crop of young shallots with the individual bulbs just beginning to form.**

traditional deterrent. In both cases you will have to burn or destroy any infected bulbs.

Various fungal diseases, such as neck rot and white rot, can affect shallots. Burn or destroy all infected bulbs.

Cultivation
Planting time late winter to early spring
Planting distance 15–18cm/6–7in
Planting depth just below the surface
Distance between rows 30cm/12in
Harvesting midsummer

Varieties

'Atlantic' yellow skinned
'Delicato' red skinned
'Dutch Red' red skinned
'Dutch Yellow' yellow skinned
'Giant Red' red skinned
'Giant Yellow' yellow skinned
'Golden Gourmet' yellow skinned
'Hâtive de Niort' brown skinned
'Pikant' yellow skinned
'Sante' yellow skinned
'Success' red-brown skinned
'Topper' yellow skinned

shallots

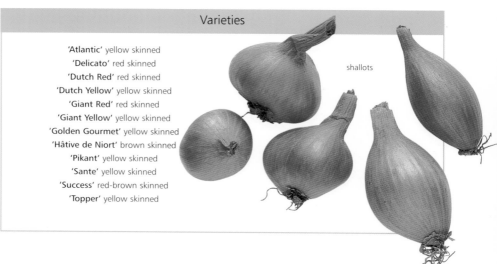

Spring Onions (Scallions)
Allium cepa

Spring onions (scallions) are small onions that are eaten fresh; they are not dried. They produce small bulbs that are little more than a slight swelling at the base of the stem. The bulb and the base of the stem is white; the cylindrical leaves are green. A young form of large, bulbous onions, they originate from the same part of the world, Central Asia. They are called spring onions (scallions) because they are ready to eat in spring, unlike other onions, which do not mature until later in the year.

ABOVE **Spring onions (scallions) can be pencil-slim or have a slight swelling at the base, forming a small bulb.**

The Welsh onion is similar to spring onions (scallions) but derives from a different species, *Allium fistulosum*. It has little to do with Wales, since it has been introduced to the West only relatively recently, although it has been in cultivation in China since prehistoric times. It found its way westwards through Russia in the early 17th century, possibly picking up its name from the German *welsche* (foreign) on the way. Welsh onions are somewhat coarser in appearance than spring onions. They are perennials, rather like coarse chives, and the foliage can be used in the same way as that of chives.

Bunching onions are similar again and have been derived from Welsh onions. These can be used as annuals, like spring onions (scallions), or as perennials, like Welsh onions.

Spring onions (scallions) can be used in cooking but they are more frequently eaten raw, especially in salads. The leaves can be used as a substitute for chives, and the onions themselves are often used as a garnish. Welsh and bunching onions are used in much the same ways.

Many gardeners use shallots for pickling. However, there is also a special type of pickling onion (also called a cocktail onion) that can be grown. These are similar to spring onions (scallions) except that the bulb develops more fully. They are small, white-skinned onions. Like spring onions, they are grown from seed sown in the spring and are usually ready for harvesting after two months. They are treated in the same manner as spring onions and can be left unthinned for smaller bulbs or thinned for larger ones. The smaller ones can be used as a substitute for bulbous spring onions. Although usually pickled they can be stored like other bulbous onions.

Cultivation

Like the rest of the family, spring onions (scallions) need an open, sunny site. The soil should preferably be light, but they will grow in most soils as long as they are manured. Dig in manure in autumn for spring sowing. Sow the seed in spring and then at three-week intervals for a succession. Late summer sowings can be overwintered under cloches for an early spring crop.

Sow thinly in drills 1cm/½in deep and 15–20cm/6–8in apart. If sown thinly enough, there should be no need to thin. This is important because the smell of bruised plants that is caused by thinning attracts onion fly.

Spring onions (scallions) should be grown quickly or they become tough, so they will need watering in dry weather. Welsh onions are grown in the same way but should be left in situ – only the leaves are cropped. Lift and divide every few years when the clumps get congested.

Harvesting

Spring onions (scallions) are ready for use at about eight weeks from sowing. Simply pull them from the ground. If the soil is compacted, they can be eased out with a hand fork.

Storage

Spring onions (scallions) cannot be stored for more than a few days. Keep in a cool place or in a refrigerator. The leaves can be chopped

THINNING ....

Although it is advisable to avoid thinning spring onions (scallions) where possible, it is often necessary to thin out congested rows.

HARVESTING ....

Spring onions (scallions) can be harvested either by pulling them from the ground by hand or, as is shown here, by gently forking them out.

and frozen, either in bags or in ice cubes, for use in winter in the same way as chives.

ABOVE **Spring onions (scallions) that have been newly harvested.**

Pests and diseases

The main pest is onion fly, whose maggots eat the onions, turning the leaves yellow and eventually killing them. The dangerous period is when the onions are damaged by thinning or weeding because the flies smell the odour that is given off. Burn or destroy any affected onions. Onion eelworm produces distorted leaves. Again, burn or destroy affected plants.

Various fungal diseases can affect spring onions (scallions) but because their life is so short any diseased plants should be destroyed and a fresh start made in a new position in the garden.

Cultivation

Sowing time early spring
Sowing distance sow thinly
Sowing depth 1cm/½in
Distance between rows 15–20cm/6–8in
Thinning distance avoid thinning if possible
Successional sowing three-week intervals
Harvesting eight weeks after sowing

spring onions (scallions)

Varieties

'Guardsman' for summer use
'Hikari Bunching' for summer use
'Ishikura' for summer use

'North Holland Blood Red' red skinned, for summer use
'Santa Claus' red skinned, for summer use
'Savel' for summer use
'White Knight' for overwintering
'White Lisbon' for summer use and overwintering
'Winter White Bunching' for overwintering

Leeks

Allium porrum

Like most forms of onion, leeks have been grown since ancient times. They were probably derived from Allium ampeloprasum, which grows in the Near East and in countries of the Mediterranean littoral. Its traditional connection with Wales arose because Welshmen were said to have worn leeks in their hats in a battle against the Saxons in AD640 to distinguish them from their enemies.

Although leeks belong to the onion family, they do not have such a pronounced basal swelling nor the pungent flavour and smell of the other culinary members of the genus. They consist of cylinders of tightly wrapped leaves, white where they have been blanched and green above soil level. It is the white section that is mainly used. Unlike the other culinary onions, which are mainly used as flavourings, leeks are used as a vegetable in their own right in a wide range of dishes and soups. They can also be used, of course, as a simple vegetable accompaniment.

A wide range of varieties is available, some are hardier than others (those with bluer leaves tend to be hardier), and some are

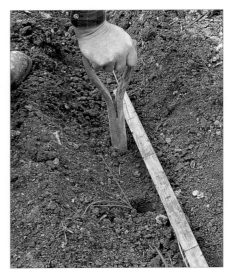

1 Make a hole with a dibber and drop the plant in. Do not fill in the hole.

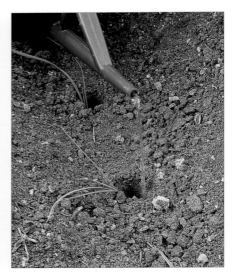

2 Fill each hole along the row with water.

ready earlier, while others stand better until spring. Some varieties have been bred specifically for their appearance on the show bench.

Cultivation

Leeks like an open, sunny position and a rich, fertile soil that is reasonably free draining. Dig well-rotted organic compost into the soil in autumn for planting in spring. Leeks like a long growing season, so start them off by sowing in nursery-bed rows in early to mid-spring. Sow thinly in drills 1cm/½in deep and 15cm/6in apart if you need more than one row. Transplant

BELOW **A good block of leeks, with their rich green leaves, looks decorative in its own right.**

Cultivation

Sowing time early to mid-spring
Sowing distance sow thinly
Sowing depth 1cm/½in
Distance between sown rows 15cm/6in
Planting distance 15cm/6in
Distance between planted rows 30cm/12in
Harvesting early autumn to late spring

when the seedlings are 15–20cm/6–8in high, which will be two or three months after sowing. Water the row the day before lifting and then dig out in batches with a hand fork. Plant into their permanent rows using a dibber. The plants should be 15cm/6in apart and the rows should be 30cm/12in apart. Make a hole about 15cm/6in deep and drop the leek in so that about 5cm/2in of the leaves show above the soil. Do not fill in the hole with soil, but fill it with water. This will wash sufficient soil around the roots.

As the leeks grow, earth (hill) them up by pulling soil up around the stems to blanch them. Alternatively, plant the leeks in the bottom of a trench and gradually fill the trench as the leeks grow. Keep weeded and watered in the early stages of growth.

Harvesting

Leeks can be lifted for use at any time between early autumn and late spring. Dig them out with a fork. Autumn varieties are not as hardy and should be harvested before midwinter.

Storage

Leeks are generally hardy and can be left in the ground until they are required. In cold areas they can be covered over with a cloche. They are best used fresh from the ground, but they can be dug several days before use and kept in a cool place. There is no method of storing leeks out of the ground. If the piece of ground they occupy is needed for some other purpose in the spring, then they can be lifted and heeled in elsewhere until they are needed. Simply dig a trench and insert the leeks to the same depth as they were in their original planting position. Dig them up as and when they are required.

EARTHING (HILLING) UP

Earth up the plants as they grow in order to blanch the stems. Alternatively, plant the leeks in a trench and fill it in as the plants grow.

Pests and diseases

Leeks are not usually troubled by pests and diseases. Rust is the most likely problem. Infected plants can be burned or destroyed; if the rust is not too severe it can be ignored, although it is best to plant leeks elsewhere for the next year. Other onion pests and diseases may occasionally be a problem; destroy any affected plants.

Varieties

Autumn
'Albinstar'
'Autumn Giant Startrack'
'Autumn Mammoth-Argenta'
'Elephant'
'Pancho'
Mid-season
'Carentan'
'Cortina'
'Grenvilliers-Splendid'
'King Richard'
Winter
'Alaska'
'Giant Winter-Cantalina'
'Giant Winter-Royal Favourite'
'Giant Winter-3'
'Kajak'
'Musselburgh'
'Wila'
'Yates Empire'

HARVESTING

Harvest the leeks by digging under them with a fork. As you do this, pull them from the ground with the other hand.

leeks

LEAF VEGETABLES

Cabbages

Brassica oleracea Capitata Group

Cabbage has been in cultivation for 3,000 years or so, but the cabbage as we know it today is a comparatively recent development, probably dating from the Middle Ages. Cabbage can be found growing in the wild throughout Europe, from Britain to Spain, but the wild form is more akin to broccoli than the hearted varieties with which we are now familiar.

Cabbages come in various forms, mainly depending on the time of year they are harvested – spring, summer, autumn and winter varieties are self-evidently named. These are all hearting cabbages, although spring cabbage is also available as "greens", which are loose heads of green leaves, unlike the typical tight heads of blanched leaves. There are also a few other winter varieties, which are sometimes considered separately, such as the savoys (with their distinctive, crinkly leaves), hybrids between the savoys and winter cabbages and 'January King'. The most distinctive of this group of cabbages is the red cabbage.

Some people have been put off cabbage by having to eat overcooked leaves, but it has always remained a staple winter vegetable for gardeners, especially in country areas, and nowadays it is enjoying a revival in popularity as people increasingly appreciate its culinary potential.

Cultivation

Cabbages do best in an open, sunny site in a soil that is fertile but reasonably free draining. They do not like a soil that is too acid, and acid soil may need liming to bring it to pH6.5–7. This should be done immediately after digging and before planting. Most gardeners sow cabbages in nursery beds and transplant them; others prefer to sow them in trays under glass; still others buy them as young plants from nurseries and garden centres. The methods are basically the same for all types; it is just the timing that varies.

Thinly sow seed in shallow drills about 1cm/½in deep. Thin seedlings if necessary to prevent them from becoming drawn. After about five weeks, when they have four or five leaves, transplant them to their final position. Final spacing depends on the type and size (see Cultivation). Plant using a dibber or trowel and firm the soil in well around the roots. Water well and keep watered until they have become established.

Spring cabbages can be sown in situ and initially thinned to 10cm/4in. In spring thin again to 30–38cm/12–15in.

Hoe regularly and keep free of weeds. Draw up some soil around the stems of over-wintering varieties. Remove any dead leaves.

Harvesting

Cut the hearting cabbages when they have become firm. Use a knife to cut through the stem, just below the firm head but inside any loose leaves. Savoy cabbages taste better if they are harvested after they have experienced at least one frost. The leaves of spring cabbages are cut as required, a few being left to heart up if required.

Storage

Most cabbages are winter hardy and can be left where they are until required. Those with solid heads can be cut and stored in a cool place, where they will keep for a couple of months. Some varieties of red cabbages may not be as hardy and can be harvested in early winter and stored.

PROTECTING YOUNG CABBAGES

Young cabbages need protecting from birds. Wire guards are light and easy to erect. They are also easy to store if they are made in short sections.

PREVENTING CABBAGE ROOT FLY

Cabbage root fly can be kept at bay by placing a felt or plastic collar around the base of the cabbage in order to stop the fly laying its eggs.

Cultivation

Spring cabbage
Sowing time late summer
Sowing distance sow thinly
Sowing depth 1cm/½in
Distance between sown rows 15cm/6in
Planting distance 30–38cm/12–15in
Distance between planted rows 50–60cm/20–24in
Harvesting spring

Summer cabbage
Sowing time early to mid-spring
Sowing distance sow thinly
Sowing depth 1cm/½in
Distance between sown rows 15cm/6in
Planting distance 35cm/14in
Distance between planted rows 60cm/24in
Harvesting midsummer onwards

Autumn cabbage
Sowing time late spring
Sowing distance sow thinly
Sowing depth 1cm/½in
Distance between sown rows 15cm/6in
Planting distance 50cm/20in
Distance between planted rows 60–75cm/24–30in
Harvesting autumn

Winter cabbage
Sowing time late spring
Sowing distance sow thinly
Sowing depth 1cm/½in
Distance between sown rows 15cm/6in
Planting distance 50cm/20in
Distance between planted rows 60–75cm/24–30in
Harvesting winter

Varieties

Spring cabbage
'April'
'Durham Early'
'Greensleeves'
'January King'
'Offenham 1-Myatt's'
'Offenham Compacta'
'Pixie'
'Spring Hero'

Summer cabbage
'Castello'
'Derby Day'
'Hispi'
'Minicole'
'Primo'
'Quickstep'

Autumn cabbage
'Autoro'
'Bingo'
'Castello'
'Minnicole'
'Rapier'
'Winnigstadt'

Winter cabbage and savoys
'Best of All'
'Capriccio'
'Celtic'
'Christmas Drumhead'
'Duncan'
'Hidena'
'Ice Queen'
'January King'
'Novusa'
'Ormskirk 1-Ormskirk Late'
'Tundra'
'Wivoy'

Red cabbage
'Kissendrup'
'Metro'
'Red Drumhead'
'Red Dutch'
'Ruby Ball'
'Vesta'

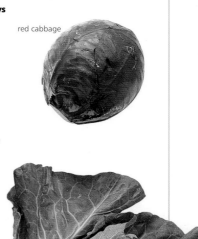

red cabbage

loose-leaf cabbage

Pests and diseases

Cabbage root fly are a nuisance, but they can be deterred by placing a collar of roofing felt or a similar material around the plant's stem. This prevents the adults from laying their eggs near the plant. Caterpillars are another problem. Cover the plants with netting or fleece to stop butterflies laying their eggs. Caterpillars can be removed by hand, but if you decide to spray, follow the manufacturer's instructions. Flea beetles make small holes in young leaves and should be prevented by dusting with the appropriate chemical. Slugs and snails should be controlled. The most serious disease is club root, which causes the roots to swell up. Any affected plants should be burned or destroyed. Liming helps to deter club root, as does growing cabbages in a different bed each year.

RIGHT **A block of cabbages in very good condition.**

Brussels Sprouts
Brassica oleracea Gemmifera Group

Brussels sprouts are so called because they are thought to have originated in Belgium, where they are recorded as growing in the mid-18th century. By the beginning of the 19th century they had spread to France and Britain. Even after 200 years of cultivation, Brussels sprouts still seem to be an acquired taste. Not everybody likes them, and children in particular seem to find that they have too strong a taste. When cooked properly, however, they are a very tasty and valuable part of winter meals, and few would consider their Christmas dinner complete without a bowl of them.

Brussels sprouts are usually categorized according to season: early, mid and late. If plants are grown from each group, there can be a continuous crop from autumn right through to spring.

The sprouts themselves are the tight buds that form where the leaves join the main stem. As well as the sprouts, the succulent tops of the plants can be harvested once the sprouts are finished. The size of the plant varies according to cultivar, and some that have been bred as dwarf or compact plants are best suited to smaller gardens where space is at a premium. Another intriguing type is the red-leaved variety, 'Rubine', which is ideal for decorative kitchen gardens.

ABOVE These Brussels sprouts are just beginning to develop. Soon the lower leaves will be removed, exposing the sprouts.

Cultivation

An open position is required, but it should be protected from strong winds. The ground should be manured in autumn and limed if necessary to bring the acidity to within pH6.5–7. The seed can be sown in the open ground or started in trays under cover. For a late-summer picking, the seed should be sown in late winter or early spring – soil and weather conditions would generally mean that these seeds should be sown inside. For the more usual autumn-onwards harvest, sow in the open in early to mid-spring. Sow the earliest varieties first and the latest a few weeks later to make sure that they crop successionally. Sow thinly in shallow drills (see Cultivation). Plant out in the final position about five weeks after sowing, when the plants are about 13cm/5in tall. Plant the taller varieties at 75cm/30in intervals and the dwarfer forms at 50cm/20in intervals, with 75cm/30in between rows. Use a dibber or a trowel and firm the soil lightly around the plant. Water well.

Keep the plants well watered until they are established. Because there is such a large amount of space between plants they can be intercropped with a fast-growing crop such as radishes or lettuces. Keep the weeds down. If the site is exposed, stake the plants against the wind, and drawing soil up around the stems also helps. Remove the bottom leaves as they turn yellow.

Harvesting

Harvest when the Brussels sprouts are large enough to pick but while they are still tight. Start at the bottom of the plant, picking a few off each plant and snapping off each one with a downward twist. Move up the stems as the sprouts fill out. When all the sprouts are removed, pick the loose heads or tops and cook them as greens. Most gardeners prefer not to start harvesting until after the first frosts because this improves the flavour. As you harvest, remove any sprouts that have "blown" – that is, those that have not formed tight sprouts but are just a loose collection of leaves – and put them on the compost heap.

BELOW Here, purple-leaved Brussels sprouts make an impromptu, but striking, combination with *Dahlia* 'Bishop of Llandaff' on the other side of the fence.

Cultivation

Sowing time early to mid-spring
Sowing distance sow thinly
Sowing depth 1cm/½in
Distance between sown rows 15cm/6in
Planting-out time when 13cm/5in high
Planting distance 50-75cm/20-30in
Distance between planted rows 75cm/30in
Harvesting mid-autumn to spring

Storage

Brussels sprouts are hardy and can be left on the stems until they are required. They cannot be stored after picking for any length of time unless they are frozen. Freeze early maturing varieties before the weather damages the outer leaves. Choose only good quality, uniform sprouts for freezing.

Pests and diseases

Brussels sprouts are prone to the same problems as cabbages. The worst problem is clubroot. Aphids will also take shelter in the tightly packed sprouts.

ABOVE **This healthy block of Brussels sprouts has been planted with red cabbages to create a highly decorative effect.**

Brussels sprouts

Varieties	
Early	'Mallard'
'Lancelot'	'Roger'
'Oliver'	**Late**
'Peer Gynt'	'Fortress'
Mid-season	'Icarus'
'Bedford Fillbasket'	'Sheriff'
'Citadel'	'Trafalgar'
'Evesham Special'	'Widgeon'

Cauliflowers

Brassica oleracea Botrytis Group

Cauliflowers are not the easiest of crops to grow, but they are one of the most rewarding, both in a sense of achievement and in the eating. Like so many of our vegetables, their origins are rather obscure. The Romans are thought to have cultivated a type of cauliflower, but the vegetable as we know it today originated in the countries at the eastern end of the Mediterranean at a much later date. It was introduced into Italy in the late 15th century and finally reached Britain about a hundred years later. However it was another two hundred years before it came to be widely grown.

Cauliflowers are characterized by their large, dome-shaped heads of creamy-white flowers (which are generally known as "curds"). When well-grown, these should be tight, evenly shaped and unblemished. The typical cauliflower has creamy-white curds, but there are also other colours for those who want something a bit different. Purple is the most common alternative colour, but there are also various shades of green and orange, although most of these are not true cauliflowers but hybrids, often produced using broccoli. The heads are usually 15–20cm/6–8in across, but there are now modern hybrids, often known as mini-cauliflowers, which develop very quickly and have heads to only 10cm/4in or less across.

Cauliflowers must be firmed in well when they are planted. Plants in loose soil run to seed quickly.

For those with the space to grow them there are cauliflowers for almost every season of the year. The only gap comes in winter, because most of the so-called winter cauliflower are not, in fact, ready until spring.

Cauliflowers can be awkward to grow, but, with care and attention, all gardeners should be able to produce good-quality crops. The main factor is to make sure that the plants' growth is not checked, because this causes irregular and undersized curds. An irregular water supply can be one cause. Late transplanting may be another. The one aspect that is difficult for the gardener to control is high summer temperatures, which are not conducive to growing good cauliflowers, since they prefer cool conditions. In hot areas you may have to abandon the idea of summer cauliflowers and concentrate on winter varieties.

Cultivation

Cauliflowers should be planted in an open, sunny position. To grow cauliflowers well it is essential that you have a fertile soil, preferably manured during digging in autumn. The manure is important, because the soil should be moisture-retentive so that the plants are not checked during dry

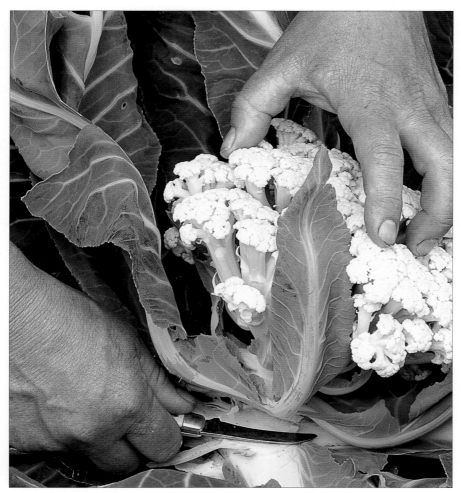

LEFT **Harvest the cauliflower by cutting the stem with a sharp knife just below the first ring of leaves.**

periods. The soil must not be too acid; if possible adjust the pH level to 6.5–7 by liming in autumn.

Cauliflowers can be sown in the open ground or in modules or trays. They should be sown thinly in shallow drills about 1cm/½in deep and 20cm/8in apart. For the timing for the various seasons, check the Cultivation box. If necessary, thin the seedlings to about 5cm/2in apart. Transplant them when they have five leaves, which should be about six weeks after sowing. Water the rows of seedlings on the day and then transplant them using a dibber or trowel. Firm the soil around the plant down well with your heel. The planting distances vary from 50–75cm/20–30in, depending on the variety: compare Varieties with Cultivation box.

Keep cauliflowers well watered, especially in warm, dry spells. Once the curds begin to form, snap the larger outside leaves down over them to protect them. This will prevent discoloration.

Harvesting

The curds are ready when they form an even dome shape. Summer and autumn varieties mature in about 16 weeks from sowing and winter ones in about 40 weeks. Mini varieties are ready in about 15 weeks. When they are ready, cut through the stem with a sharp knife just below the head, leaving one or two leaves around the curd to protect it on its way to the kitchen. If you are storing them for a while, cut them so

cauliflower

PREVENTING SUN SCORCH

Protect the curds from discoloration by the sun by covering them with the inner leaves.

that they have a short length of stem from which you can hang them. If the leaves are occasionally sprayed with water, they will keep for several weeks in cool conditions.

Storage

In general, it is best to leave the cauliflowers on the plants until they are required, but they can be cut and placed in a cool place for up to three weeks. They store best if they are hung upside down, otherwise cauliflowers will freeze well.

Pests and diseases

Cauliflowers are susceptible to the same problems as cabbages.

Cultivation

Early summer
Sowing time midwinter
Sowing position under glass
Planting-out time spring, when 13cm/5in high
Planting distance 50cm/20in
Distance between planted rows 60cm/24in
Harvesting early to midsummer
Summer
Sowing time mid-spring
Sowing distance sow thinly
Sowing depth 1cm/½in
Distance between sown rows 20cm/8in
Planting-out time early summer, when 13cm/5in high
Planting distance 60cm/24in
Distance between planted rows 60–75cm/24–30in
Harvesting late summer
Autumn
Sowing time late spring
Sowing distance sow thinly
Sowing depth 1cm/½in
Distance between sown rows 20cm/8in
Planting-out time early summer, when 13cm/5in high
Planting distance 60cm/24in
Distance between planted rows 60–75cm/24–30in
Harvesting autumn
Winter
Sowing time late spring
Sowing distance sow thinly
Sowing depth 1cm/½in
Distance between sown rows 20cm/8in
Planting-out time summer, when 13cm/5in high
Planting distance 70–75cm/28–30in
Distance between planted rows 60–75cm/24–30in
Harvesting late winter to early spring
Mini-cauliflowers
Sowing time spring
Sowing distance station sow 15cm/6in
Sowing depth 1cm/½in
Distance between sown rows 45cm/18in
Harvesting late summer to autumn

Varieties

Early summer and summer	Late summer and autumn	Winter
'All Year Round'	'All Year Round'	'Arcade'
'Alpha'	'Autumn Glory'	'Cappacio'
'Mayflower'	'Castlegrant'	'Early Feltham'
'Montana'	'Dok Elgon'	'Jerome'
'Snow Crown'	'Plana'	'Purple Cape'
'Snowball A'	'Violet Queen'	**Mini-cauliflowers**
'White Summer'	'Wallaby'	'Candid Charm'
		'Mini-Cauliflower King'

Spinach

Spinacia oleracea

Spinach is the bane of most children and many adults, and yet when it is cooked properly it is a magnificent vegetable and a key ingredient in many classic and modern dishes. Spinach is related to the beetroots (beets) and chards and not to the cabbages or lettuces, to which it bears a superficial resemblance. It was first cultivated in Asia by the Persians, and it spread along the trade routes to China and eventually to Spain by the 11th century. It was five centuries later that it arrived in Britain.

S pinach is really a plant for a cool climate. It dislikes hot, dry summers, when it will very quickly go to seed, often before it is fully developed and ready to harvest. However, if you make sure that your plants are properly watered and that you select cultivars that suit your area, you can produce a crop that should last for two or three weeks and, with successional cropping, this can be extended considerably.

The plants look rather like a loose lettuce, with stalked leaves rising from a central stem. When the plant bolts, this stem quickly elongates. Supplying the plant with plenty of moisture and nourishment can postpone the tendency to bolt.

Alternatives to spinach

Spinach has a relatively short life, especially in hot, dry summers, when it is likely to bolt, and so many gardeners (erroneously one can't help feeling) think it is not worth growing. There are other vegetables that are cooked in the same way as spinach and have the advantage of having a longer season. These are generally known as "perpetual spinach", and the

chief of them is Swiss chard. Another good alternative is New Zealand spinach (*Tetragonia tetragonioides*), which is not related botanically to spinach but makes a good substitute, both in the garden and kitchen. It is grown as an annual, but unlike true spinach it can be picked throughout the summer months and also way into autumn. Sow in trays or modules under glass and plant out after the danger of frosts has passed. Alternatively, station sow at 45cm/18in intervals in shallow drills, 1cm/½in deep, where they are to grow, again after the last frosts. It is more tolerant of drought than spinach but it does best if watered during dry periods. Pinch

HARVESTING

Spinach is a very easy crop to harvest. When you require some, simply cut away the young leaves with a pair of sharp scissors.

LEFT **This beautifully maintained walled potager includes a healthy crop of spinach.**

out the tip to make it bush out and harvest the leaves when they are big enough. Carry on doing this for as long as the plants last. Do not allow them to set seed or they may self-sow and possibly keep coming up for several years.

The young leaves of red orache or red mountain spinach (*Atriplex hortensis*) can also be used in the same way. In spring, sow seed where they are to grow either in shallow drills or by broadcasting. Thin to 30cm/12in apart. It is worth growing in a potager for its decorative qualities alone.

Cultivation

Grow spinach in an open, sunny position but preferably one that does not get too hot. The soil should be fertile and contain as much organic material as possible so that it is moisture retentive. Permanently wet soils should be avoided, however. Dig in manure or compost in autumn.

Thinly sow the seed in early spring, with successional sowings at two-week intervals through to late spring. It is better to sow several short or part-rows at intervals than one long one if there is the possibility that most of the plants will run to seed before they are harvested. Sow in shallow drills, about 1cm/½in deep and 30cm/12in apart. As soon as the seedlings are big enough to handle, thin them out to 15cm/6in apart. Keep well watered and keep weeds under control.

A crop for overwintering can be sown in late summer or early autumn. This will benefit from being covered with cloches from autumn onwards. The cloches will not only protect the plants, but will keep the leaves tender.

Harvesting

Start harvesting as soon as the leaves are big enough, which is usually 8–12 weeks after sowing. Don't strip the plant, but just take a few leaves to start with and until the plants are mature. Break or cut the stems, but avoid pulling because this may loosen the plant and precipitate bolting. Continue harvesting until the plants start to run to

seed – when the central stem starts to elongate. When harvesting winter spinach, do not overpick.

Storage

Spinach should be picked and used as fresh as possible because it does not store. The leaves can, however, be frozen.

Pests and diseases

Spinach should be grown so fast that there can be few problems (apart from

bolting) and, in any case, there is little time for the gardener to satisfactorily correct any problems that do occur. The best solution in this case is to scrap the affected plants and start again.

To avoid slug damage, clear the ground of slugs before sowing and at regular intervals thereafter.

The most likely diseases to affect spinach are downy mildew (choose resistant varieties) and spinach blight. Destroy the affected plants.

Varieties	
Summer	**Winter**
'Bloomsdale'	'Broad-leafed Prickly'
'King of Denmark'	'Norvak'
'Long Standing'	'Sigmaleaf'
'Medana'	'Symphony'
'Monopa'	
'Melody'	
'Triathlon'	

spinach

Lettuce
Latuca sativa

Lettuce is an odd vegetable, which is as often used for decorative purposes as for taste and nutrition. Shop-bought lettuces have much to answer for in this respect, as are the oft-repeated scare stories about their being full of chemicals. Home-grown lettuces not only have flavour, but you also know what they have been fed on. Another advantage of growing your own lettuces is that you can grow several different types and colours so that you can make a really attractive salad – and, of course, they are fresh. You can pick just as many leaves as you want right at the last minute.

Lettuces have been popular for a long time and were even depicted in carvings and paintings in Ancient Egypt. They were popular among the Romans, who are reputed to have introduced them to Britain. The original lettuces were probably quite bitter and needed blanching to make them palatable, much like endives today.

Modern gardeners are fortunate in having so many different types as well as a wide range of varieties. The main type is the cabbage or headed lettuce. These are either loose balls of soft leaves – butterhead lettuces – or those with much firmer, crinkly-edged leaves – crispheads. Cos or romaine lettuces are more upright and have long, crisp leaves and a succulent heart. Then there are the loose-leaved or non-heading varieties, which do not produce a heart but just a mass of loose, individual leaves. These lettuces are very good when you want to be able to take leaves as and when you require them. There has recently been a great deal of interest in these

HARVESTING

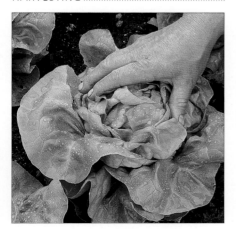

Harvest lettuces when the "heart" feels firm.

cut-and-come-again lettuces, and many new varieties have appeared. This method of growing lettuces is far from new, however.

The mainstay of salads, lettuce is usually eaten raw, although an increasing number of recipes include cooked lettuce. Lettuce leaves are also widely used as a garnish, for which the coloured forms of the loose-leaved varieties are particularly useful. There is now quite a wide range of red- and bronze-leaved forms, as well as green forms with decorative leaves.

Lettuces are not difficult to grow and, in theory, can be harvested all year round, but some type of protection is required for winter varieties. They grow relatively quickly and will be ready from 5 to 12 weeks after sowing, depending on the variety. This means that they can be grown among slower growing crops or used to replace another crop that has already been harvested.

Cultivation
Lettuces need an open, sunny position, although light, partial shade during the heat of the day can be an advantage in hot areas or during hot summers. The soil needs to be fertile and, preferably, moisture retentive, and this is best achieved by incorporating plenty of manure during the autumn dig. Lettuces can be sown straight in the ground or grown in trays and transplanted. It is a good idea to sow a short row of lettuces and then, instead of throwing away the thinnings, to transplant them to make up the rest of the row. The advantage of this is that the trans-plants will take a few days to settle down and will produce a slightly later crop than the sown plants. If the whole row is sown at once, the lettuces will mature at the same time, which will probably mean that many are wasted.

ABOVE **A block of developing lettuces shows how decorative this varied crop can be.**

Transplanting is difficult after midsummer, because lettuces often rapidly run to seed.

Start early sowings in trays or modules under glass in late winter or early spring. Plant these out under cloches or in cold frames to get an early crop. Seed can be sown directly in the soil from early spring onwards. Sow in shallow drills 1cm/½in deep, each row about 30cm/12in apart. Thin the lettuces to 15–30cm/6–12in apart, depending on the size of the variety. Transplanted lettuces should be planted at the same distances. Keep the soil moist and do not allow the plants' growth to be checked or they will rapidly run to seed. Sowings after midsummer will provide lettuces for autumn and early winter, but cover them with cloches when necessary from around mid-autumn. Special winter varieties can be overwintered under cloches or grown in greenhouses or in cold frames.

Harvesting
Lettuces can be harvested whole or leaves can be taken from the plants as required. The loose-leaved varieties are usually picked leaf by leaf, but cabbage-type varieties can be picked in the same way if you wish. Hearted varieties are usually ready for harvesting as soon as they feel plump and firm. Do not leave them too long in the

ground after maturing or they may bolt. Pull the whole lettuce from the ground or cut below the bottom leaves if you want the plant to resprout. Loose-leaved varieties mature earlier, and leaves can be picked as soon as they are large enough, which is usually from about seven weeks after sowing.

Storage

Whole lettuces can be kept in a refrigerator for a short time, but they are best used straight from the garden.

Pests and diseases

Slugs and greenfly (aphids) are two of the worst problems and should be dealt with by your preferred methods. Other pests can include root aphids and cutworms.

The main disease is downy mildew, and lettuces also tend to suffer from a few other fungal diseases. These occur mainly in wet seasons and are best avoided by making sure that individual lettuces are not planted too close together. This will ensure that there is plenty of air movement around the

ABOVE **A block of decorative lettuces, showing the rich variety of colours available.**

plants. If pests or diseases do get out of control, do not spend a lot of time and money on chemical control. Simply get rid of the plants and start again.

Cultivation

Sowing time late winter (under glass) to early spring onwards
Sowing distance thinly
Sowing depth 1cm/½in
Distance between sown rows 30cm/12in
Thinning distance 15–30cm/6–12in
Harvesting early summer onwards

Varieties

Butterhead	Cos	'Lobjoits Green Cos'	'Lollo Rosso'
'Avondefiance'	'Balloon'	'Paris White'	'Red Fire'
'Buttercrunch'	'Bubbles'	'Wallop'	'Red Sails'
'Continuity'	'Corsair'	**Loose-leaved**	'Redina'
'Dolly'	'Little Gem'	'Cerise'	'Salad Bowl'
'Hilde II'		'Cocarde'	**Winter**
'Musette'		'Frisby'	'Arctic King'
'Sabine'			'Kellys'
'Tom Thumb'			'Novita'
Crisphead			'Valdor'
'Avoncrisp'			'Winter Density'
'Beatrice'			
'Iceberg'			
'Lake Nayah'			
'Malika'			
'Minetto'			
'Saladin'			
'Warpath'			
'Webb's Wonderful'			

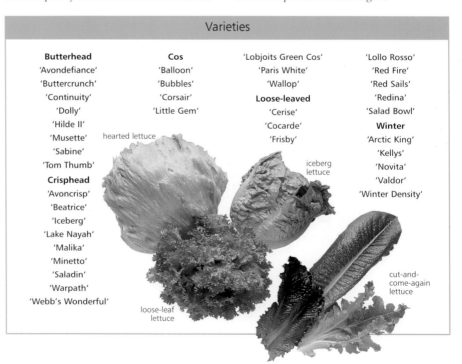

hearted lettuce

iceberg lettuce

loose-leaf lettuce

cut-and-come-again lettuce

Salad Leaves

Although lettuces, perhaps supplemented by leaves such as endives and chicory, provide the traditional greenery for most salads, there is an increasing number of small leaves that play their part. Some are available during the winter months, when lettuce from the garden may be scarce, and as well as adding bulk, each adds an individual flavour to pep up the overall interest of the salad. The two most important of these salad leaves are rocket (arugula; Eruca vesicaria), which is also known as salad rocket, rucola and Italian cress, and lamb's lettuce (mâche; Valerianella locusta), which is also known as corn salad.

Neither rocket (arugula) nor lamb's lettuce (mâche) is new – indeed, both have been eaten for centuries – but their popularity seems to be on the increase, particularly in the United States, where numerous varieties are available. The choice is also increasing in Europe, where it has always been particularly popular in France, from where many of the varieties come.

Young rocket (arugula) leaves have a sharp taste, and the older the leaves, the hotter and spicier the taste. They are usually eaten raw in salads, but older leaves are sometimes cooked, and the flowers can be eaten too. They make an excellent winter crop. Lamb's lettuce (mâche) is also used as a winter crop. The leaves are milder than those of rocket, and it is also much slower growing, taking up to 12 weeks before being ready to cut, compared with three weeks for rocket.

Several other leaves can be grown, each needing similar cultivation to rocket (arugula) and lamb's lettuce (mâche). The leaves of land cress (*Barbarea verna*) have a similar flavour to watercress. Mustard (*Brassica hirta*) and the similar tasting salad rape (*Brassica napus*) are also worth growing. Cress (*Lepidium sativum*), also known as garden or curly cress, can be grown to complement the other leaves, and winter purslane (*Claytonia perfoliata*) is another mild leaf for the salad bowl.

ABOVE **Chinese leaf mustard, in this case the variety is 'Red Giant', will add a zing to any salad with its pungent flavour.**

Cultivation

All these salad leaves are plants for a cool climate and will rapidly run to seed in hotter areas. Because of this and because other salad materials are scarce at that time, they are mainly grown for autumn and winter use. In cooler areas they can be sown in spring for summer use. Although they are hardy, they need to be protected by cloches to be at their best.

Both rocket (arugula) and lamb's lettuce (mâche) are sown in late summer; rocket can also be sown in early autumn. Sow in drills 1cm/½in deep and 30cm/12in apart. Thin the resulting seedlings to 15cm/6in apart for rocket and 10cm/4in for lamb's lettuce. Keep lettuces watered if the weather is dry. Cover with cloches in late autumn or early winter.

LEFT **Land cress, often known as upland cress, is similar in taste to watercress and is often used as a land-grown substitute. This makes a welcome contribution to most salads.**

Cultivation

Rocket (arugula)
Sowing time late summer to early autumn
Sowing distance thinly
Sowing depth 1cm/½in
Distance between sown rows 30cm/12in
Thinning distance 15cm/6in
Harvesting late autumn onwards

Lamb's lettuce (mâche)
Sowing time late summer
Sowing distance thinly
Sowing depth 1cm/½in
Distance between sown rows 30cm/12in
Thinning distance 10cm/4in
Harvesting winter

Harvesting

Either pick individual leaves or cut off the lot as soon as they are large enough. They will sprout again.

Storage

Both plants should be picked as required because they will not store.

Pests and diseases

Both plants should be free of both pests and diseases, although rocket (arugula) may be attacked by flea beetle. If the tell-tale marks appear on the leaves, dust with derris.

Varieties

Rocket (arugula)
Sold under one or other of its common names – rocket (arugula), rucola, salad rocket – rather than as varieties.
Lamb's lettuce (mâche)
Frequently sold simply under its common name.
'Cavallo'
'Grote Noordhollandse'

'Jade'
'Verte de Cambrai'
'Volhart'

ABOVE **Curled cress, or simply cress, is grown for its sprouts, but can also be used when fully grown, as is the case here.**

rocket (arugula)

lamb's lettuce (mâche)

LEFT **Lamb's lettuce or mâche is a mild-flavoured leaf that is useful in autumn and winter salads.**

ROOT CROPS

Parsnips
Pastinaca sativa

Parsnips were developed in Europe from the widespread wild parsnip. It is possible that the Greeks and Romans cultivated them, but there is confusion over whether they were referring to parsnips or carrots in their writings. However, parsnips were certainly being eaten in Europe in the Middle Ages, although they subsequently went into something of a decline (except as cattle food), and it is principally in Britain where they remain popular. Parsnips have always been part of country fare, but they are now regaining a rightful place as vegetables for discerning palates.

There is not much to see of the parsnip above ground, except for its inedible leaves. It is the large, swollen root that is the part that is eaten. Some varieties, especially when they are in light, fertile soil, can grow very big, to 45cm/18in or even longer. For most purposes, however, smaller roots are more than adequate.

There are more than 30 different varieties of parsnip. They differ little from each other, although some are more resistant to canker, while others have less hard cores. Certainly, none is more decorative than any other, either in the garden or on the plate. Ultimately, your choice of variety will be based on which grows best for you and which taste you prefer, although, in truth, there is not a great deal of difference.

Cultivation

An open, sunny position is required. Parsnips can be grown in heavy soils, but they prefer light ones, and although they do best in a fertile soil, do not sow them on freshly manured ground (the parsnips fork). Sow in soil that was manured the previous season or dug in the autumn. Always use

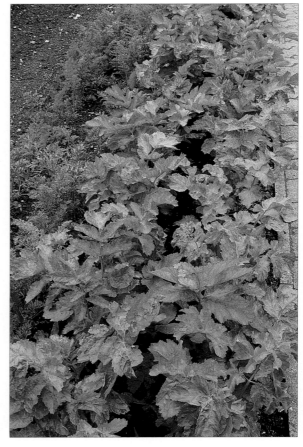

ABOVE **Parsnips can be left in the ground until they are required.**

fresh seed; last year's is unlikely to germinate. The seed should be station sown at 15–20cm/6–8in intervals in 1cm/½in drills. The rows should be 30cm/12in apart. Do not sow too early – the soil should be at least 7°C/45°F – but they do need a long growing season, so sow as soon as you can. Parsnips are slow to germinate so sow a few radishes between the stations of parsnips. These will appear quickly and mark the line of the rows, making it easier to hoe without accidentally disturbing the germinating parsnips.

In heavy or stony soils the parsnips may fork and produce stunted growth, rather than the desired conical shape. To avoid this, make holes with a crowbar at each sowing station, moving it in a circle to make an inverted conical hole in the ground. Fill this with potting compost (soil mix) or good loam and sow the seeds in this.

Thin the seeds to one to each station as soon as they are big enough to handle. Keep

PLANTING IN STONY GROUND

1 At the required sowing intervals, make an inverted conical hole with a crowbar.

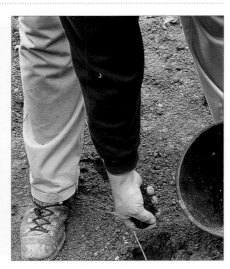

2 Fill the hole with potting compost (soil mix) and sow in the centre, covering the seed with more compost.

Cultivation

Sowing time early spring
Sowing distance station sow at 15–20cm/6–8in
Sowing depth 1cm/½in
Distance between sown rows 30cm/12in
Harvesting late autumn until spring

free from weeds. Water in dry spells
because sudden rain after a prolonged dry
spell may cause the roots to split. In very
cold climates cover the rows of parsnips
with straw during the winter.

Harvesting

Parsnips can be harvested from autumn
onwards. Although they can be harvested
before the leaves die back, most gardeners
wait for this. Many gardeners also wait until
after the first frosts, because these make
parsnips taste sweeter. Dig the roots from
the ground with a fork. In heavy soil or if
the parsnips have deep roots, take care or
the fork may slash through the flesh rather
than lifting it out of the ground.

Storage

Parsnips are very hardy and should be left
in the ground until they are required. If a
frosty spell is forecast, however, it can be a
good idea to lift a few while you can still get
them out of the ground, and place them in
trays of just-moist peat (peat moss) or sand
until they are required. They are a late crop
and may be harvested in spring well beyond
the time that the ground may require
preparing for the next crops. The parsnips
can be dug up and temporarily heeled into
another piece of ground or stored in sand
or peat as described.

Varieties

'Avonresister' small, some canker resistance	Improved' long-rooted
	'Intermediate' small
'Bayonet' long-rooted, some canker resistance	'Tender and True' long-rooted, some canker resistance
'Cobham Improved Marrow' medium	
'Gladiator' long-rooted, some canker resistance	'White Gem' medium, long-rooted
'Hollow Crown	'White Spear' long-rooted

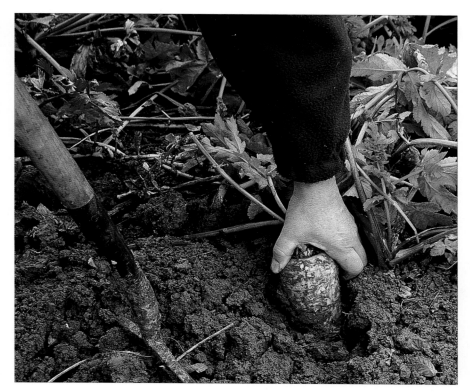

Pests and diseases

Parsnips can be attacked by such pests
as celery fly or carrot flies, but on the whole
they are usually pest free.

Parsnips are also prone to canker, but
you can help reduce the chances of this
occurring by choosing one of the increasing
number of varieties that have been grown
with a resistance to this problem.

SOWING

Parsnips are best station sown in groups of three,
eventually reducing the seedlings to one by thinning
out the weakest.

ABOVE **Harvest parsnips by digging a fork well
under the root and levering them out.**

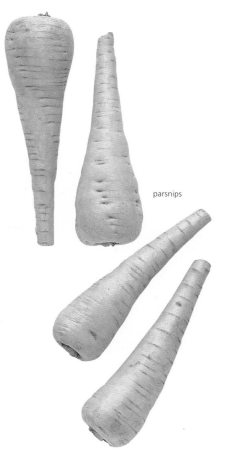

parsnips

Carrots
Daucus carota

Many people may wonder if it is worth growing carrots when they are so cheap to buy. The answer must be an emphatic "yes". Fresh carrots, whether old or young, that are taken straight from the ground before being cooked taste infinitely better than shop-bought ones; there is no comparison. You may have to put up with them being covered in mud and perhaps with slug and carrot fly holes in them, but this is a minor consideration compared with the superior taste.

Wild carrots appear throughout Europe and well into Asia. The exact origin of domestic carrots is rather obscure, but they probably originated in the countries of the eastern Mediterranean, possibly even in Afghanistan. The original domesticated ones were various colours, including white, yellow, purple and red, and carrots of these colours are currently being re-bred and will soon be re-introduced by seed merchants. The orange ones, with which we are all familiar, were developed in Holland and France at a much later date.

The edible part of the carrot is below ground, while above are the attractive filigree leaves. Although mainly grown for the kitchen, they are well worth growing as purely decorative plants.

Although carrots bought in supermarkets are more or less identical, there is a lot of variety available to the gardener. Not only are there early carrots (often grown in frames) that are round, looking almost like radishes, there are some that are long and tapered. Others are just as long but are cylindrical, with parallel sides and a rounded end. Shorter varieties are best for immediate use, while the longer ones are better for storing over winter. Although the other colours are being bred, the majority of carrots are the familiar orange, but there are a few pale yellow and creamy-white forms available.

Cultivation
Choose an open, sunny position. Carrots will grow in heavier soils, but they do best in light ground – sandy soils are perfect. The soil should be free from stones and fresh manure because both will cause the carrots to fork. If the soil is stony, make individual holes with a crowbar, fill them with compost (soil mix) and sow into these. Avoid freshly manured soil by using a plot that was manured for a previous crop or by manuring in the autumn. Sow very thinly in drills 1cm/½in deep and set 15–20cm/6–8in apart. Sow under cloches in late winter or in the open from early spring, but not before the soil has warmed up to at least 7°C/45°F. Sow successionally, with the last sowing in early summer.

When the seedlings appear, thin the earliest to 8cm/3in and the maincrop to 5–8cm/2–3in apart, depending on the size of carrot required. It is best to thin on a muggy, windless evening in order to avoid attracting carrot fly. For the same reason, remove all thinnings and bury them in the compost heap. Weed regularly but avoid disturbing the young carrots – a mulch of grass cuttings will help keep weeds down. It will also help to keep the soil moist. Water in dry weather.

THINNING

Thin the carrots only if necessary. Do so on a still, muggy evening to prevent the smell of the carrots travelling and betraying their presence to carrot root flies. Water after thinning.

Carrots must be sown thinly. To help with this mix the seed with a little silver sand and "sow" the mixture.

Harvesting
Harvesting can begin at a very early stage as the thinnings can be very delicious, although they are rather tedious to clean. Early carrots can be dug up from late spring onwards, approximately seven weeks after sowing. Maincrop carrots take a bit longer and are ready from ten weeks onwards. Shorter varieties can be pulled, but longer ones and those that have been grown in heavier soils will need digging out with a fork.

HARVESTING

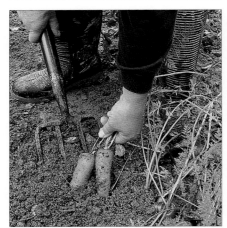

Shorter varieties can be pulled out by hand, but longer ones and those grown on heavier soils will need digging out with a fork. Try to avoid piercing the roots with the tines of the fork.

Storage

Carrots are usually left in the ground until they are required. They may even be left in the ground over winter unless there are a lot of slugs or the winter is very harsh. Instead, they can be lifted, cleaned and placed in a tray of just-moist sand or peat (peat moss).

Pests and diseases

The worst pest is undoubtedly carrot fly, the maggots of which burrow into the carrots. There are an increasing number of varieties that are resistant to this pest and these may be worth trying. Be careful when thinning, because the flies are attracted by smell, and the bruising of any part of the carrot will release the tell-tale odour. Planting garlic nearby is a traditional way of disguising the smell. Another, cumbersome but success-ful, method is to erect a fine mesh barrier, up to 90cm/3ft high, around the carrots. This deflects the flies, which fly quite close to the ground.

The principal disease from which carrots are likely to suffer is violet root rot, in which, as its name suggests, the root rots, becoming a violet colour. Burn or destroy all affected plants and make sure that you do not use the same ground for carrots for at least a couple of years.

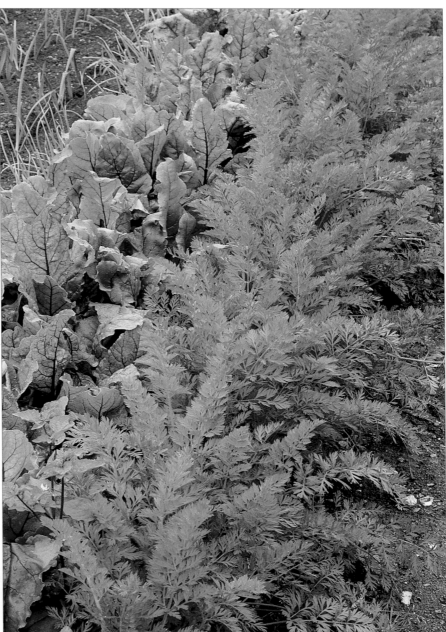

ABOVE **A flourishing row of carrots, coming to maturity. These will be ready for harvesting a few at a time, whenever required for the kitchen.**

carrots

Cultivation

Sowing time early spring and successionally to early summer
Sowing distance very thinly
Sowing depth 1cm/½in
Distance between sown rows 15–20cm/6–8in
Thinning distance 5–8cm/2–3in
Harvesting late spring onwards

Varieties

Early	'Chantenay Red Cored'
'Amsterdam Forcing 3'	tapered
cylindrical	'Favourite' stump-rooted
'Amsterdam	'Fly Away' cylindrical
Sweetheart' cylindrical	'Ingot' cylindrical
'Early Nantes'	'James Scarlet
stump-rooted	Intermediate' tapered
'Rondo' round	'Nantes' stump-rooted
Maincrop	'Nantes Express'
'Autumn King'	stump-rooted
cylindrical	'St Valery' tapered

Beetroot (Beets)

Beta vulgaris

Beetroot (beets) originated around the shores of the Mediterranean and was spread northwards into the rest of Europe by the Romans. Once the Romans reached northern and eastern Europe, the vegetable seems to have been taken to heart, and many of the recipes in use today come from these areas.

Beetroot (beets) is related closely to Swiss chard and shares its distinctive bright red coloration. This is not only manifest in the leaves and stems of the plant but also in the roots themselves, and when they are cut or bruised they exude a wonderfully deep red juice. When it is cooked, the flesh is still a very deep colour, even though it loses a lot of colour in the water if it is boiled (baking preserves it). Not everyone likes this coloration, because it has a tendency to stain not only other food, but lips and clothes as well.

However, although you never see them in greengrocers, there are also white and golden varieties, which are equally delicious but do not cause the staining. There are also a few fancy ones in which the roots are made up of concentric rings

of white and red flesh. The general shape is round or near round, but cylindrical or even tapered varieties are available.

The green or reddish-green leaves can also be eaten when they are young, either in salads or cooked.

Unlike parsnips and carrots, the bulk of the vegetable's swollen root sits on top of the ground so that you can watch its progress and easily determine when it is ready to harvest.

Many of the older varieties have a tendency to bolt, particularly if they are sown early, but there are now ample alternatives that have had this characteristic bred out of them. Another aspect of choosing varieties is related to germination. Most seed is, in fact, made up of a cluster of seeds, which means that when they germinate they produce several seedlings close together. However, if you find that thinning these is fiddly, look out for monogerm varieties, which usually have the word "mono" somewhere in their name.

BELOW **Beetroot growing in a block in a raised bed. This method enables you to control the growing medium and grow crops unsuited to your soil.**

Cultivation	
Sowing time early spring and successively to early summer	
Sowing distance thinly or in stations at 8cm/3in intervals	
Sowing depth 1cm/½in	
Distance between sown rows 20cm/8in	
Thinning distance 8cm/3in	
Harvesting early summer onwards	

Cultivation

Beetroot (beets) needs an open, sunny position. They will grow in heavy soils, but do best in light ones. The soil should be fertile but not freshly manured. Use a plot that was manured for the previous crop or one into which manure was dug during the

HARVESTING

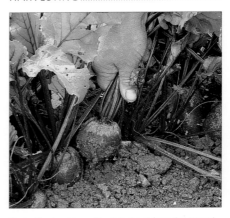

Harvest beetroot by pulling it by hand from the ground. In heavier soils a fork may be needed to loosen the roots.

PREPARING FOR COOKING

Remove the leaves by twisting them off, 3–5cm/1–2in from the root. This prevents the beetroot (beets) losing their colour by "bleeding" when they are cooked.

previous autumn. Sow directly into the open soil into shallow drills 1cm/½in deep and set 20cm/8in apart. The seed should be station sown at 8cm/3in intervals or sown thinly and thinned to that distance when they have germinated. Beetroot (beet) seed is slow to germinate but it can be speeded up by soaking for an hour in warm water before sowing. Seed can be sown in early spring, once the soil has warmed up to 7°C/45°F, and successively sown at two-week intervals until early summer. An earlier sowing can be made under cloches.

Keep beetroot (beet) weed free but avoid damaging them with a hoe. Keep them supplied with constant moisture. Avoid alternating dry and wet periods, or they may split.

Harvesting

Pull the young beetroot (beets) from the ground while they are still quite small. This will be about seven weeks after sowing. Continue to pull as required. You may need to use a fork to help ease later crops or those in heavy soils from the ground. If possible, do not break the thin root attached to the bottom of the globe, because this will "bleed", causing the beetroot to lose a lot of its colour. For a similar reason do not cut off the leaves; instead, twist them off, leaving about 5cm/2in on the beet.

Storage

Beetroot (beets) can be left in the ground until they are required, except in cold districts, where they can be lifted, cleaned and placed in trays of just-moist sand or peat (peat moss). Store these trays in a cool, frost-free shed or garage.

Pests and diseases

On the whole, beetroot (beets) are reasonably trouble free in terms of possible pests and diseases. Birds may eat the young

seedlings when they first appear, so keep these off with netting of some sort. If any diseases occur, burn or destroy the affected plants and re-sow them elsewhere.

ABOVE **Even a small garden such as this can accommodate a selection of crops, including onions and beetroot (beets).**

Varieties

'Action' miniature
'Albina Vereduna' white flesh
'Boltardy' round
'Burpee's Golden' gold flesh
'Cheltenham Green Top' cylindrical
'Cheltenham Mono' monogerm
'Chioggia Pink' pink and white stripes
'Cylindra' cylindrical
'Detroit-Little Ball' miniature
'Dorée' golden
'Forono' cylindrical
'Moneta' monogerm
'Monodet' monogerm
'Monogram' monogerm
'Monopoly' monogerm
'Red Ace' cylindrical
'Tardel' miniature

purple beetroot (beets)

white beetroot (beets)

golden beetroot (beets)

Swedes (Rutabagas or Yellow Turnips)

Brassica napus

Swedes are one of those vegetables that never seem to get into ready-prepared, convenience dishes and yet are still popular with cooks who prepare their own food. They belong, perhaps, to what one might call the category of "wholesome food" (such as stews) rather than high cuisine, but they are increasingly used in a wide range of dishes, including delicate soups. Swedes are convenience food in their own right – it takes only a matter of seconds to pull one from the ground, peel, chop and put it to cook.

Swedes (rutabagas or yellow turnips) are not very old as vegetables go, although no one is certain about their origins. It seems likely that they appeared in Europe as a random cross between turnips and cabbages sometime in the Middle Ages. They did not find their way to Britain until the latter part of the 18th century, and it is thought that they were introduced from Sweden, hence the name. The American name "rutabaga" also has Swedish origins, being derived from *rotbagga*, which is Swedish for "ram's foot", an apt visual description of small or immature swedes.

Cultivation	
Sowing time late spring to early summer	
Sowing distance thinly	
Sowing depth 1cm/½in	
Distance between sown rows 38cm/15in	
Thinning distance 23cm/9in	
Harvesting autumn onwards	

Although they are usually considered a rootcrop, swedes (rutabagas or yellow turnips) actually belong to the cabbage family and, as such, suffer from similar pests and diseases. For this reason, they should be included with the cabbages when you are planning a rotational system. The swollen root of the swede is mainly above ground, with just a small amount being buried. In the better garden varieties, the top of the globe is usually purple, while the lower section, which is hidden from the light, is white. The flesh is a creamy-yellow, usually deepening during cooking. The appearance of the foliage clearly shows its close alliance to the cabbage.

Many gardeners used to sow a later crop of swedes (rutabagas or yellow turnips) around midsummer in order to provide "tops", or the leaves, which can be used as greens during spring. These can be grown closer together than suggested above for conventional use.

Cultivation

An open site is required. Like most root crops, swedes (rutabagas or yellow turnips) prefer a light soil, although they can be grown on heavier ground. As with most brassicas, the soil should not be too acid. Lime if necessary to bring it to about pH6.5. The ground should not be freshly manured, but it is important that it contains as much organic material as possible because the soil should be moisture retentive. Add manure during autumn digging. Sow thinly in late spring or early summer into drills that are 38cm/15in apart and 1cm/½in deep. Thin the swedes

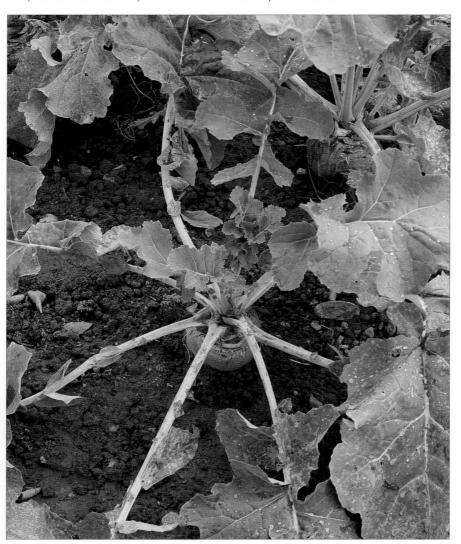

LEFT **This is a typical swede, with lots of spreading leaves. This plant should stand in the ground throughout the winter.**

ABOVE **These healthy looking swedes have just been harvested. The spreading stems can be clearly seen. This variety is 'Acme'.**

RIGHT **Swedes are generally round, but can vary in shape depending on the growing conditions. This variety, 'Marian', has become elongated.**

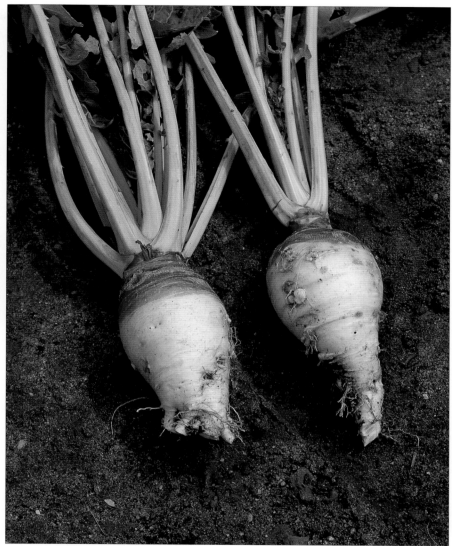

to 23cm/9in apart, preferably doing this in stages. Make sure that the soil is kept moist throughout summer, otherwise any check in the growth may result in woody or split globes. Keep the weeds down.

Harvesting

Swedes (rutabagas or yellow turnips) can be harvested from autumn onwards, throughout the winter, once they are large enough to use. Lift the globes as they are required. In most soils they can simply be pulled from the soil, but in heavier ones they may need loosening with a fork first.

Storage

Swedes (rutabagas or yellow turnips) are completely hardy and can be left in the soil as long as necessary. Some varieties become woody if they are left in the ground beyond the turn of the year, however, so these should be lifted and stored in trays of just-moist sand or peat (peat moss) and placed in a cool, frost-free shed or garage.

Pests and diseases

Being brassicas, swedes are prone to the same diseases as the rest of the cabbage family. Flea beetles are a particular scourge and the leaves should be dusted with derris as soon as they are spotted. Mildew can also be a problem, but there are now varieties that are resistant. Club root is another problem to look out for.

purple-topped swedes (rutabagas or yellow turnips)

Varieties	
'Best of All'	'Marian'
'Brora'	'Ruby'
'Devon Champion'	'Western Perfection'

Turnips
Brassica napa Rapifera Group

Like swedes (rutabagas or yellow turnips), turnips are members of the cabbage family. The origins of the turnip go back so far that they are obscure, but the wild plant from which it is derived is still commonly found throughout Europe and Asia and is thought to have been cultivated as far back as prehistoric times. The long history has meant that many forms have appeared in cultivation, particularly in China and Japan. The popularity of the turnip has waned in the West, and with it a number of different forms, although there are still some 30 varieties from which to choose.

The Western form of the turnip is round, sometimes an almost perfect globe, sometimes slightly flattened. It has one thickish root or several roots emerging from the base. The skins are a creamy-white, and the top of the globe can be green, purple, white or creamy-yellow. The flesh is white or yellowish. The globe is partly sunk into the ground, but most of it is above ground. In Asia long-rooted varieties are also grown, and seed of this form is sometimes available in the West. It is also possible sometimes to find old European varieties with long roots.

The fleshy ball is cooked and eaten, but many gardeners also enjoy the young leaves, which are cooked as spring greens. Summer turnips are more succulent and lend themselves to a range of dishes. Those that are overwintered are generally not quite as tender, but they are useful in casseroles, stews and soups. In Japan they are often eaten raw.

Cultivation

Because turnips are a member of the brassica family, they should be included with cabbages in the rotational sequence. They need an open, sunny situation and, preferably, a light soil, although they can be grown in heavier ground. There must be plenty of organic material in the soil so that it does not dry out. The manure should either be left from a previous crop or be dug in during the previous autumn.

Cultivation

Summer
Sowing time late winter (under cloches) to early spring
Sowing distance thinly
Sowing depth 1cm/½in
Distance between sown rows 23cm/9in
Thinning distance 13cm/5in
Harvesting summer

Autumn and winter
Sowing time mid- to late summer
Sowing distance thinly
Sowing depth 1cm/½in
Distance between sown rows 30cm/12in
Thinning distance 20cm/8in
Harvesting autumn and winter

Greens
Sowing time late summer
Sowing distance thinly
Sowing depth 1cm/½in
Distance between sown rows 8–10cm/3–4in
Thinning distance none
Harvesting spring and early summer

Sow early varieties of turnip under cloches in late winter for early crops or in open ground from early spring onwards. Sow seed 1cm/½in deep in drills 23cm/9in apart. When the seedlings are big enough to handle, thin them to about 13cm/5in apart. Continue to sow at two- to three-week intervals for a continuous

BELOW **A well-shaped, purple-topped turnip. It is advisable to keep turnips moist so that they will grow quickly.**

HARVESTING

Turnips can be harvested by simply pulling them from the ground.

ABOVE **These turnips – a variety known as 'Tokyo Cross' – have just been harvested and will grace any dining table.**

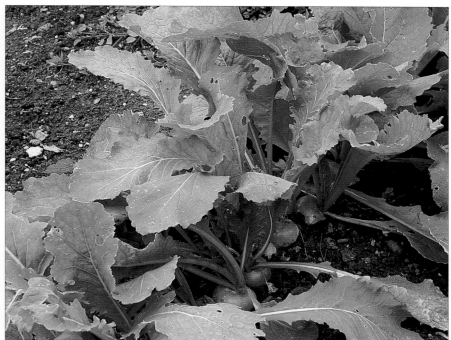

ABOVE **The distance between the plants in this row of red-topped turnips is just right for growing them successfully.**

supply of small, tender turnips throughout the summer. For varieties to be harvested from the autumn and winter, sow in midsummer. They should be at the same depth, but rows should be about 30cm/ 12in apart. Thin the seedlings to 20cm/8in.

If you want to grow turnips just as "greens", sow thinly in late summer and there should be no need to thin. Rows can be as close as 8–10cm/3–4in.

The secret of growing good turnips is to keep them moist so that they can grow quickly. Keep them weeded.

Varieties	
'Golden Ball'	'Milan White
'Green Top Stone'	Forcing'
'Hakutaka'	'Orange Perfection'
'Imperial Green	'Presto'
Globe'	'Purple Top Milan'
'Jersey Navet'	'Red Milan'
'Manchester Market'	'Snowball'
'Market Express'	'Stanis'
'Milan Early	'Stone'
White Top'	'Tokyo Cross'
'Milan Purple	'Tyfon'
Top Forcing'	'Veitch's Red Globe'

Harvesting

Harvest the early and summer varieties as soon as they are the size of golf balls. They can be eaten when they are slightly larger, but they are at their best at this size. Larger and older turnips become woody, so rather than sowing one long row, it is better to sow short rows at different times to provide a steady supply of young turnips. Varieties sown in midsummer can be harvested from autumn onwards as they are required. The "greens" can be harvested as young leaves from spring into summer.

Storage

Turnips can be left in the ground until they are required. In very cold areas or if they are likely to be frozen in the ground and impossible to extract, they can be lifted, the tops removed and the globes stored in trays of just-moist sand or peat (peat moss), and kept in a frost-free place.

Pests and diseases

Turnips suffer from the same problems as cabbages. Flea beetle, which is likely to be the worst pest, should be treated with derris dust.

Diseases can include violet root rot and club root. Destroy any affected plants.

green-topped turnips

Potatoes
Solanum tuberosum

The potato is one of the most important food crops in the world. The family to which it belongs, Solanaceae, is found worldwide, although the potato itself originates from a fairly restricted area in the Andes, spreading up into Mexico. There are many species involved in the botanical development of the potato, which is very complicated, and the history of the potato in cultivation is almost as complicated as its botanical history.

The potato has been grown as a vegetable in the Andes for thousands of years, and the Incas were discovered to be eating it by the conquering Spanish in the late 16th century. Taken to Italy, it eventually spread to the rest of Europe. The original cultivars were not particularly hardy, and it took a long time for the potato to catch on in northern Europe and two centuries before it was widespread in Britain.

The tubers – that is, the swellings on the roots – are eaten. All other parts, including the leaves and the fruit, are poisonous. If the potatoes themselves are exposed to light for any length of time, they turn green, and this, too, is poisonous unless cooked.

Potatoes are grown from "seed potatoes". These are not seeds in the conventional sense, but potato tubers that have been selected for growing. Once they have been planted, the seed potatoes start to sprout, producing roots and leaves. As the roots grow, new tubers are formed on them, and these are harvested when they are large enough.

Because potatoes are so widely distributed, there are hundreds of varieties from which to choose. Many are suited to particular climates, and different types will be found in different countries. The varieties differ in a number of respects. The first main difference is the timing of the crop, and there are two main groups, earlies and maincrop, which are further subdivided into first earlies and so on. The next main difference is use. Some are better for baking or roasting; others are better for boiling or frying; others are suitable for salads.

ABOVE **Potatoes have attractive flowers. In early crops, the opening of the flowers is an indication that the tubers are ready.**

Finally, and in some respects the most important criterion, is flavour. Most varieties taste quite different from each other, and many gardeners have their own favourites, although this does not stop them from experimenting with different ones.

Given these characteristics, it might be supposed that gardeners would grow several cultivars. However, potatoes can

LEFT **This row of potatoes shows the earth drawn up around the stems.**

BELOW **A crop of newly dug salad potatoes, "drying" in the sun.**

Cultivation

First earlies
Planting time early spring
Planting distance 30cm/12in
Planting depth 10–15cm/4–6in
Distance between rows 45cm/18in
Harvesting early summer
Second earlies
Planting time mid-spring
Planting distance 38cm/15in
Planting depth
10–15cm/4–6in
Distance between rows 60cm/24in
Harvesting summer onwards
Maincrop
Planting time mid- to late spring
Planting distance 38cm/15in
Planting depth 10–15cm/4–6in
Distance between rows 75cm/30in
Harvesting autumn

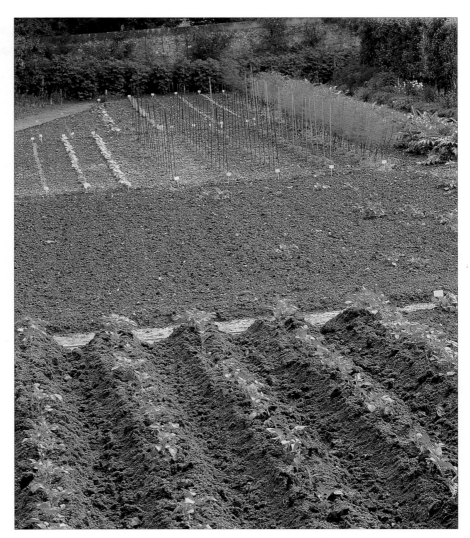

ABOVE **This large kitchen plot contains rows of neatly earthed- (hilled-) up potatoes. Frosts can be a problem for the emerging foliage.**

take up a lot of space in the garden and they are relatively inexpensive to buy. Many gardeners, therefore, prefer to restrict themselves to growing a few earlies, which have an incomparable flavour when taken straight from the ground to the kitchen, and to go to the greengrocer for the rest of the year. The ground on which the earlies were grown can be used for later crops, such as cabbages or leeks.

There are so many varieties that it could take more than one gardening lifetime to get through them all by sowing one or two varieties each year. One way of trying as wide a range as possible is to get together with two other gardeners and to buy bags of, say, three potatoes each and to divide them up between yourselves so that each of you can grow a small number of nine

varieties rather than a large number of three varieties. Keep a note of those you like best and make them your maincrop for the following year.

It is possible to enjoy new potatoes at Christmas too by planting a few in large pots in early autumn and keeping these in the greenhouse.

Cultivation

Potatoes are best grown in an open, sunny position. As earlies are likely to emerge through the ground before the last of the frosts, try to choose a warm, protected spot away from frost pockets. They will grow on most soils, although they prefer slightly

LEFT **A recently harvested uprooting of red-skinned potatoes, all evenly shaped and with good-quality skin.**

acid conditions. The soil should be fertile but avoid planting potatoes on newly manured grounds.

Earlies should be chitted. This involves standing the seed potatoes on a tray so that the eyes are facing upwards. Place the tray in a cool but frost-free place that is in the light although out of direct sunlight. Short shoots will appear, and this gets the crop off to a good start. Maincrop can be treated in the same way, although it is not essential.

First earlies are planted in early spring followed by second earlies two weeks later. Draw out a row with a hoe about 10cm/4in deep and place potatoes at 30cm/12in intervals. Rows should be 45cm/18in apart.

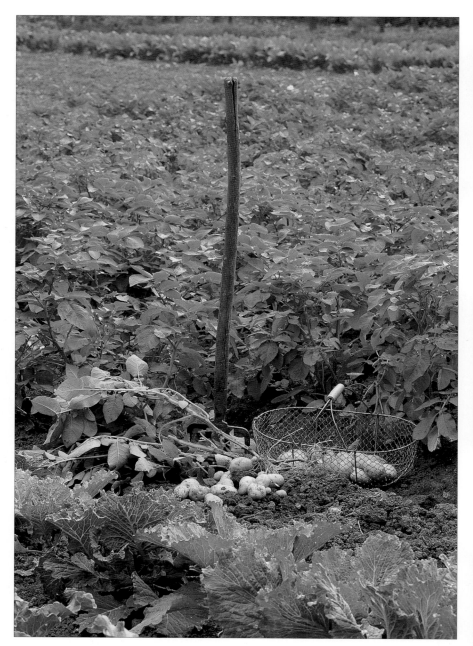

ABOVE **This harvesting of early potatoes is now ready for transferring to the kitchen. They will make delicious "new potatoes".**

Alternatively, the potatoes can be planted in holes dug with a trowel or with a special potato planter. Whichever method you use, cover the potatoes with soil and then draw up more soil to form a low ridge above them. When the shoots reach heights of 23–25cm/9–10in, draw earth up around them along the rows to make certain that all the tubers are well covered; otherwise they turn green. Continue to do this until the foliage touches across the rows.

Second earlies and maincrop are treated in the same way, except that they are planted in the second half of spring and the potatoes are set 38cm/15in apart and in rows 60cm/24in apart for second earlies and 75cm/30in apart for maincrop.

Keep an eye on weather reports, and if frost is forecast cover any shoots with newspaper or horticultural fleece. Keep all potatoes, especially earlies, watered if there is a prolonged dry spell forecast.

CHITTING POTATOES

Before planting, place the potatoes in a tray in a light place (but out of direct sunlight) in order to "chit". This means that the potatoes produce shoots.

PLANTING

Hoe out a trench 10cm/4in deep and lay the tubers about 30–40cm/12–15in apart, depending on the type. Cover with soil and earth (hill) up into a low ridge.

EARTHING UP

When the shoots reach 23–25cm/9–10in long, draw the soil around them along the rows.

An alternative method of growing potatoes is to plant them under a sheet of black polythene (plastic). Place the polythene along the row and anchor it by burying the edges in the soil. Cut slits at the relevant intervals and plant potatoes through them.

FROST PROTECTION

Once the potato shoots have emerged through the soil, it is important to take note of any frost forecasts. The shoots will need protecting from possible frost damage. Cover them over with horticultural fleece or even with newspaper.

HARVESTING

To harvest, dig a fork well under the potatoes and draw it up through the soil, bringing the tubers up with the earth.

Varieties

First earlies
'Arran Pilot' white skin, early
'Epicure' white skin, early
'Foremost' white skin, waxy yellow flesh
'Maris Bard' white skin, waxy texture, very early
'Pentland Javelin' white skin, waxy flesh
last of the earlies to crop
'Ulster Chieftain' white skin, floury texture

Second earlies
'Estima' white skin, waxy yellow flesh, good boiler
'Kondor' red skin, yellow flesh, good boiler
'Marfona' white skin, heavy cropper, good for baking
'Maris Peer' white skin, waxy texture, good boiler
'Wilja' white skin, waxy yellow flesh, good salad potato

Maincrop
'Cara' pink skin, white floury flesh, late
'Desiree' pinkish red skin, waxy yellow flesh, good for baking and for fries
'King Edward' pink and white skin, creamy floury texture, good for baking and roasting
'Maris Piper' white skin, floury texture, heavy cropper, good for baking
'Pentland Dell' white skin, floury texture, heavy cropper, good for baking and roasting
'Pink Fir Apple' pink skin, yellow waxy flesh, wonderful salad potato
'Ratte' white skin, yellow waxy flesh, excellent salad potato
'Romano' red skin, firm white flesh, good boiler

maincrop whites

earlies

salad

maincrop reds

salad reds

Harvesting

Early potatoes are harvested in early summer, usually just as their flowers are opening, which should be about 12 weeks after planting. They are usually lifted as they are required. Maincrop are left in the soil until the autumn and are usually all lifted at once and stored. To harvest earlies, dig a fork in well below the potatoes and lever them out of the soil, at the same time pulling on the haulm (stems and leaves). For maincrop, remove the haulm about two weeks before harvesting so that the skins on the potatoes harden. Lift the maincrop on a dry, warm day and leave them lying in the sun for an hour or two to let them dry and to harden the skins.

Storing

Do not leave potatoes in the light for too long. Pack them into hessian (burlap) or paper sacks and store them in a dark, cool but frost-free place. Alternatively, they can be stored in trays as long as no light gets to the tubers. Regularly check all potatoes and remove any that have started to rot.

Pests and diseases

The worst problem that can occur is blight, which is particularly prevalent in wet years. The leaves go yellow and brown and start to curl. Eventually the haulm seems to fall to pieces. The potatoes develop black patches, which eventually turn into a slimy, evil-smelling rot. Do not plant potatoes on

ground that was affected the year before (either from potato or tomato blight). Earth (hill) them up well to keep the spores from the tubers. If necessary, spray with the appropriate copper-based fungicide, preferably in wet years before blight appears. Look out for resistant varieties.

Another common disease is potato scab, which disfigures the surface of the tubers. To avoid it occurring, do not grow potatoes on ground that has been recently limed or manured. Other diseases include spraing, violet root rot and blackleg.

The main pests are slugs and wire-worms, both of which eat holes in the tubers. Other pests can include cutworms and potato cyst eelworms.

Radishes
Raphanus sativus

Radishes are one of the easiest and quickest of all crops to grow. The rapidity with which they appear through the soil makes them suitable for children to grow, because little patience is required, and, indeed, many gardeners' first experience of growing vegetables was with this humble plant. However, the wide range of types and varieties that are available make this a vegetable that is of as much interest to the mature gardener as to the embryonic one.

The radish has a long history as far as cultivation is concerned, having been known in Ancient Egypt. Its origins are obscure, but it probably derived from native plants found growing in Mediterranean countries. At first, varieties had long, tapering roots, originally black, later white, and these larger rooted forms are still cultivated in Europe. By the 18th century, however, the more familiar round ones with red skins began to appear.

Today the small, red-skinned radishes are the most frequently grown, and these are mainly used in salads or as a decorative garnish. In China and Japan, where the large varieties are still common, they are eaten both raw and cooked, and the large-rooted types are becoming more widely grown in the West, especially new varieties imported from China. These larger varieties

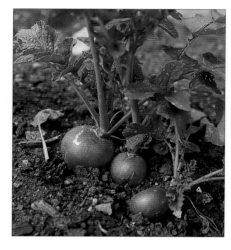

ABOVE **These round radishes are suffering from slug damage (top) and from cracking due to irregular watering (middle).**

have the advantage that they can be left in the ground for longer and so make a valuable contribution to the selection of winter crops.

One of the advantages of the short life-cycle of the radish is that it can be grown among slower growing crops, thus making the best use of the available ground. Radishes make good markers if they are sown along with a vegetable that is slow to germinate, such as parsnips. Because

BELOW **These neat rows of radishes have been planted in abundance. You will have to consume large quantities to grow so many at once.**

HARVESTING

Radishes are harvested simply by pulling them from the ground by hand. They should be harvested when they are large enough to eat.

Cultivation

Summer
Sowing time late winter (under cloches) to early spring onwards
Sowing distance thinly
Sowing depth 1cm/½in
Distance between sown rows 15cm/6in
Thinning distance 2.5cm/1in
Harvesting late spring onwards

Winter
Sowing time midsummer
Sowing distance thinly
Sowing depth 1cm/½in
Distance between sown rows 25cm/10in
Thinning distance 13cm/5in
Harvesting autumn onwards

radishes appear quickly they will indicate the position of the row so that the parsnip seeds are not accidentally disturbed by hoeing or weeding.

Cultivation

Ordinary summer radishes do not need either a deep or particularly rich soil. They prefer one that does not dry out or they will quickly run to seed. Slow-growing radishes also tend to be woody and over-hot to the taste. They should be grown in an open, sunny position.

Sowing can start under cloches in late winter or in early spring in the open soil. Sow in shallow drills about 1cm/½in deep, set about 15cm/6in apart. Water the soil along the row if it is dry at the time of sowing. Sow thinly so that little thinning is required, then thin to about 2.5cm/1in. Do not sow too much at once because radishes are rapidly past their best, and it is better to sow short rows every two weeks to obtain a succession of crops than one long one in which many of the roots will be wasted. Do not let them dry out.

Sow the larger winter radishes at about midsummer. Do not sow too early or they may run to seed. These should be sown in drills set 25cm/10in apart. When they are large enough to handle, thin to about 13cm/5in apart.

Harvesting

Summer radishes should be pulled when they are large enough to eat. Discard any that have become large or old because these will be too woody as well as too hot to eat. Winter radishes can be dug up from autumn onwards.

Storage

Summer radishes quickly shrivel once they are out of the ground and should be used as soon as possible after harvesting. Long-rooted winter varieties can be left in the ground until they are required. In very cold areas or if severe frosts are threatened, which would make digging them from the ground impossible, dig the roots and store them under cover in trays of just-moist peat (peat moss) or sand.

Pests and diseases

Although they may not look like it, radishes are related to cabbages and so suffer from the same pests and diseases. Flea beetle is likely to be the worst problem, and should they appear, young plants should be dusted with derris. Slugs are also partial to radishes and can leave unsightly holes in the roots. If anything worse than this happens, scrap the plants and re-sow elsewhere in the garden.

Varieties

Summer	'Saxa' globe
'Cherry Belle' globe	'Scarlet Globe' globe
'Crystal Ball' globe	'Sparkler 3' globe
'Flamboyant Sabina'	**Winter**
cylindrical	'Black Spanish Long'
'French Breakfast'	'Black Spanish
cylindrical	Round'
'Juliette' globe	'China Rose'
'Long White Icicle'	'Mino Early'
tapering	'Minowase'
'Prinz Rotin' globe	'Violet de Gournay'

ABOVE **A bunch of recently harvested cylindrical radishes. They should not be allowed to grow too large, or they become woody and very hot.**

radishes

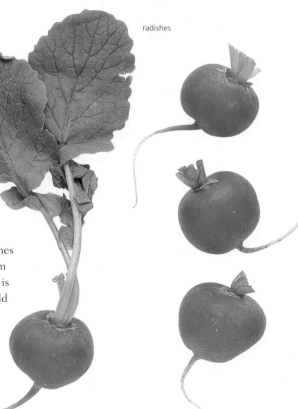

PEAS AND BEANS

Peas

Pisum sativum

Of all vegetables, peas are perhaps the best reason for growing one's own: it is impossible to buy peas that taste anything like those that are picked straight from the garden. However, the difficulty is that if you want to grow a succession of crops to give you peas throughout the summer, you will have to devote quite a large area to them. This is not the problem it once was, however, because the majority of peas are now much shorter, and even if you have space to grow only a few in a large bucket, the effort is worth it for the taste alone.

Peas are one of the oldest vegetables cultivated by man. They have been found in settlements from the Late Stone Age onwards – that is, nearly 8000 years ago. One of the advantages of peas has always been that not only can they be eaten fresh, either raw or cooked, but they can also be dried and stored for later use.

The Romans, in particular, spread the cultivation of peas, probably introducing them to Britain. Surprisingly, they seem to have vanished from cultivation in Britain and were reintroduced from mainland Europe only in the 16th century. The wild pea, from which the cultivated form was developed, is still found growing in Turkey, and it is thought that this is where they probably originated, especially as some of the earliest archaeological finds come from that area.

Until about 50 years ago, peas grew to 1.8m/6ft or more and had to be supported with pea-sticks. Modern varieties are generally quite short, however, and can be easily supported with low wire netting or even a couple of strings stretched horizontally. Some varieties need no support at all.

Although the peas themselves are generally regarded as the "vegetable", from surprisingly early – certainly before the end of the 16th century in Britain – there have been forms with edible pods. There are various types of pea. First earlies are the earliest of the year. Those that are overwintered have smooth skins, but there are less hardy varieties, which are planted in early spring, and these have wrinkled skins. Although they are less hardy, they taste sweeter. Second earlies and maincrop all have wrinkled skins.

Mangetout (snow) peas, also known as sugar peas, can be eaten whole when the peas are still immature. Snap peas also have edible pods but can be eaten when they are more mature. Asparagus peas have winged pods and an asparagus-like taste. Petit pois are small, sweet-tasting peas.

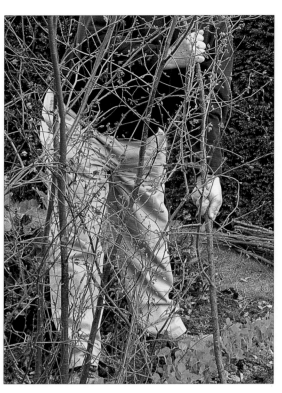

ABOVE **Pea-sticks can be used to support tall varieties of peas.**

Cultivation

Peas like an open, sunny site. The soil should be fertile, with manure or compost incorporated during the previous autumn. First earlies can be sown in late autumn and then overwintered; remember to cover the plants with cloches in colder areas. Alternatively, they can be sown in the late winter or early

SOWING

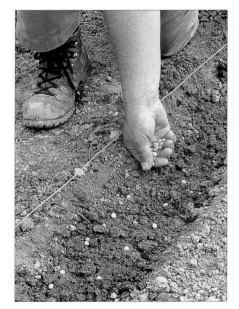

Peas can be sown in a double row along a shallow trench, in an open, sunny position.

PROTECTING AGAINST BIRDS

Covering the plant with a wire netting guard will keep the birds away.

Cultivation

Earlies
Sowing time late autumn, late winter
or early spring
Sowing distance 5cm/2in
Sowing depth 5cm/2in
Distance between sown rows 60–90cm/2–3ft
Thinning distance no need to thin
Harvesting early summer

Second earlies
Sowing time early spring
Sowing distance 5cm/2in
Sowing depth 5cm/2in
Distance between sown rows 60–90cm/2–3ft
Thinning distance no need to thin
Harvesting early summer

Maincrop
Sowing time early spring to early summer
Sowing distance 5cm/2in
Sowing depth 5cm/2in
Distance between sown rows 60–90cm/2–3ft
Thinning distance no need to thin
Harvesting summer to early autumn

spring. They can also be grown under cloches if necessary. Crops can then be sown at intervals until the early summer.

The easiest way to sow peas is to pull out a flat-bottomed trench with a hoe, about 15–20cm/6–8in wide and 5cm/2in deep. The peas are then sown in pairs, one on each side of the trench with the seeds at 5cm/2in intervals. Alternatively, they can be sown in a single drill at the same intervals. The distance between rows varies between 60–90cm (2–3ft), depending on the height of

the peas. Add supports when the peas reach 5–8cm/2–3in high and the tendrils start to form. Use plastic pea netting, which is sold specially for the purpose, wire netting or pea-sticks. Once the flowers start to appear, keep the peas watered during dry weather.

Harvesting

Pick the pods as soon as the peas have swollen and are large enough to eat. Mangetout (snow) peas and similar types should be picked before the pods get tough.

ABOVE **Wire netting can be used to support shorter varieties of peas.**

Keep picking the peas as they mature. The peas of many modern varieties, which have been created for agricultural needs, mature at the same time, and this can be a problem for the gardener.

Storage

Peas are best picked straight from the plant, although they can be frozen, which is one way of coping with a glut so that they are available through the whole year. Although it is not common now, they can also be kept by drying.

Pests and diseases

Unfortunately, peas are prone to quite a number of pests and diseases. At an early stage both mice and birds can eat the seed. Birds will also strip the emerging seedlings, and it may be necessary to protect them with wire netting. Aphids and pea thrips can also be a problem.

Mildew is something that affects crops most years, especially later in the season. It can normally be ignored, but you may prefer to use varieties that are less prone to mildew.

Varieties

Round
'Bountiful' early, tall
'Douce Provence' early, short
'Feltham First' early, short
'Meteor' early, short
'Pilot' early, medium

Wrinkled
'Alderman' maincrop, tall
'Banff' early, short
'Early Onward' early, tall
'Hurst Beagle' early, short
'Hurst Greenshaft'
maincrop, short
'Little Marvel' maincrop, short
'Miracle' maincrop, tall

'Onward' maincrop, short
'Top Pod' maincrop, medium

Petit pois
'Darfon' maincrop, short
'Minnow' maincrop, short

Mangetout
'Herault' early, tall
'Honey Pod' early, short
'Nofila' early, short
'Norli' early, short
'Oregon Sugar Pod' maincrop,
medium
'Sugar Short Sweet Green'
maincrop, medium

Asparagus pea
Usually listed by its name
rather than by variety.

mangetout
(snow) peas

round peas

round peas

Runner Beans

Phaseolus coccineus

Although many gardeners have given up growing peas because they feel they take up too much space, very few seem to have given up runner beans for the same reason. Possibly it is because they are seen as better value for money and space because they continue to crop over a long period and it is possible to freeze any excess for later use. As with peas, fresh runner beans are far better than those you buy in the shops, so the effort is certainly worthwhile.

Runner beans originated in Mexico, where they have been grown for more than 2,000 years, long before the Spanish conquistadors arrived. They were introduced to Europe in the 16th century but were at first grown more for their decorative qualities than for their culinary ones. Even today their presence in a kitchen garden is notably ornamental, although the beans are usually eaten as well as admired.

Runner beans usually grow up to about 1.8m/6ft, although in good soil they will grow to 2.4m/8ft or more. There is, how-ever, little to be gained from growing them so tall because it is difficult to harvest the topmost beans. Dwarf varieties are avail-able for those who want them, but they have never become very popular, partly because yields are lower and partly because all the beans tend to mature at the same time. The pods are long and rather coarse in texture, much coarser than the equiva-lent French (green) beans. This coarseness

also applies to the texture, and it is important to pick the pods young – once they age they become very stringy. Some varieties are less stringy than others.

The pods are usually eaten along with the young beans, but they can be allowed to mature and the fully grown beans dried and eaten later in the year.

The general colour of the flowers is red, hence the old name of scarlet runner beans, but there are now other colours, including white and mauve. These are very useful in decorative schemes, and they still produce a good crop of beans.

Cultivation

Beans do best in an open, sunny position; in more exposed areas they should be protected from winds, partly to prevent them from blowing over and partly because pollination is more difficult in such condi-tions. They will grow in quite poor soil but do best in a soil that has been well manured during the previous autumn. The tradi-tional method is to dig a deep trench and bury plenty of compost and manure, even old newspaper. The idea is not so much to provide nutrients, although this is obviously important, but to create an area around the roots that retains plenty of moisture.

Beans must not appear above ground before the last frost has passed, so early summer is usually the earliest one can begin planting. To get them off to a good start, sow beans individually in pots or modules and plant out when the weather is right. Alternatively, sow directly into the

ABOVE **This is a good crop of runner beans which is accompanied by the flowers to produce more.**

soil. If you are able to make an early start, it is often a good idea to sow again some three weeks later so that there is a continu-ous crop until the first frosts of winter.

Before sowing or planting you will need to construct some form of support up which the beans will climb. This can be in the form of a single or double row (double is usually preferable) of poles, canes or strings for them to climb up, or it can be a wigwam or tepee – that is, a circle of poles or canes, pulled together at the top with string to form a cone. The distance between the poles or strings should be about 25cm/10in, for although they will grow closer together, it is easier to pick the beans if the plants are not too close.

Plant or sow one bean at each pole. Many gardeners sow two or three beans at each position – "one for the crow, one for the slug and one for the kitchen" – and remove the weaker seedlings, leaving just one. The beans are self-clinging but may need help to go up the right pole or string, as they often seem to prefer their neigh-bour's. Make sure that the soil is always moist, especially in dry periods.

HARVESTING

Harvest the beans when they are large enough, but avoid the older, tougher beans.

Cultivation

Runner beans
Sowing time late spring (under glass)
to early summer
Sowing or planting distance 25cm/10in
Sowing depth 5cm/2in
Distance between sown rows 90cm/3ft
Thinning distance no need to thin
Harvesting late summer until first frosts

Dwarf runner beans
Sowing time late spring (under glass)
to early summer
Sowing or planting distance 15cm/6in
Sowing depth 5cm/2in
Distance between sown rows 45cm/18in
Thinning distance no need to thin
Harvesting late summer until first frosts

RIGHT **A wigwam or tepee of runner beans supported by long bamboo canes.**

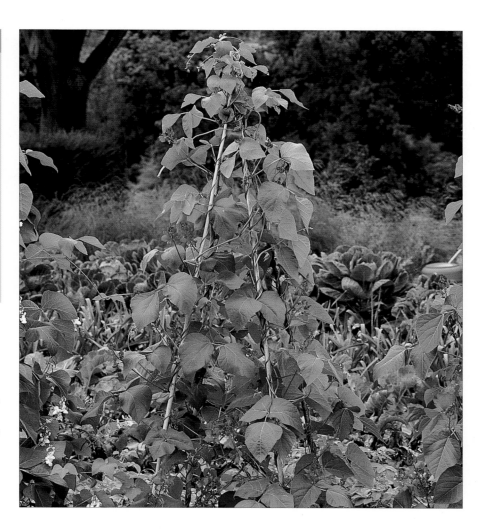

Sow or plant dwarf varieties at 15cm/6in intervals in a single row with 45cm/18in between rows. Pinch out any long shoots that develop. After harvesting, cut down the beans but leave the roots to rot in the ground; they contain stores of valuable nitrogen.

Harvesting

Pick the pods as soon as the beans begin to swell, which is usually when the beans are about 15cm/6in long. Some varieties, especially those developed for exhibition, can be considerably longer than this. A larger crop can be encouraged by picking regularly, putting any excess in the freezer. It is also important to pick regularly because old beans become stringy and inedible.

Storage

Beans do not keep well and should be eaten as they are harvested. The only storage method used today is freezing, although in the past they were often preserved in salt.

Pests and diseases

Slugs and snails are always a problem when the plants first emerge, and they can easily kill the entire planting. Runner beans are otherwise generally problem free, apart from possible attacks of blackfly.

Powdery mildew and chocolate spot may also occur.

Varieties

Runner beans
'Achievement' long pods
'Butler' stringless,
medium-length pods
'Czar' white seeds, long pods
'Desirée' stringless, long pods
'Enorma' long pods
'Ivanhoe' stringless,
lilac seeds, long pods
'Kelvedon Wonder' early, short pods
'Lady Di' long pods
'Painted Lady' medium-length pods
'Polestar' early, stringless,
medium-length pods
'Prizewinner' medium-length pods
'Red Knight' stringless
'Red Rum' early, short pods
'Royal Standard' stringless, long pods
'Scarlet Emperor' early, long pods
'Streamline' long pods
'White Emergo' white seeds, long pods

Dwarf runner beans
'Gulliver'
'Hammond's Dwarf Scarlet'
'Pickwick'

runner beans

French (Green) Beans

Phaseolus vulgaris

French (green) beans are among the oldest type of cultivated bean. They originated in Central and South America, where evidence suggests that they were being grown at least 8,000 years ago. They did not reach Europe until the 16th century, when they were introduced by the returning Spanish. The English name "French beans" presumably derives from the fact that the beans were introduced into Britain from France.

There are several distinct forms of French (green) beans, the most obvious distinction being between the dwarf and climbing varieties. Recently, climbing varieties have become a popular alternative to runner beans and this makes them seem to be a modern development, but, in fact, they are the older of the two types, dwarf beans not having been widely grown until the 18th century.

French (green) beans are either eaten whole, while the seeds are still immature, or grown on and the seeds dried and used as haricot (navy) beans. Some varieties are better for drying than others. Pods vary: they can be green, purple or yellow, and they can be round or flat. The flat varieties tend to be more succulent, and the flat ones often become rather stringy when they become old.

Like runner beans, French (green) beans are frost tender and need to be sown or planted out after the last frosts. They also need warm soil in which to germinate and thrive. They are, however, quicker to mature than runner beans and so provide a valuable early crop. They also have a quite different flavour and so bring welcome variety to the kitchen.

Dwarf varieties are still the most popular, especially as they do not take up much room and are useful in small gardens. In addition, the yield is high and the season for each sowing is relatively long. The climbers or pole varieties are a useful alternative to runner beans because of their different taste and earlier harvest and also because they do not become so stringy. The variety of coloured pods makes them valuable in the ornamental kitchen garden.

Cultivation

French (green) beans, both dwarf and climbing, need a sunny, open site. The soil should be fertile but free-draining, preferably manured during the previous autumn. An early start can be made by sowing the beans in pots or modules under glass in late spring and planting out after the threat of frost has passed. Alternatively, they can be sown directly into the soil and covered with cloches. Most gardeners, however, tend to wait until early summer and sow directly into the soil, when the conditions should be perfect. Sow in a single or double row, spacing the beans about 8cm/3in apart in rows set 45cm/18in apart. They should be planted about 4cm/1½in deep. Climbing or pole varieties should be treated in the same way as runner beans. Keep watered in dry weather.

Harvesting

Harvesting can usually begin seven or eight weeks after sowing. Pick while the seeds are still immature and go on picking for as long as the beans cook and eat well. Leave those that you want to treat as haricot (navy) beans until the pods have swollen and turned yellow. Cut the whole plants and hang them up in a dry place to complete the drying. Shell and store.

Storage

French (green) beans are best used fresh from the plant, but they can be frozen, which is a good way of dealing with a glut. Haricot (navy) beans should be dried and stored in airtight jars.

Pests and diseases

On the whole French (green) beans are not prone to many problems. Slugs and snails are the most likely nuisance, especially when the plants are first emerging, but they can also eat the pods as well. Blackfly and fungal diseases may also be a problem.

Cultivation
Dwarf beans
Sowing time late spring (under glass) to early summer
Sowing or planting distance 8cm/3in
Sowing depth 4cm/1½in
Distance between sown rows 45cm/18in
Thinning distance no need to thin
Harvesting late summer until first frosts
Climbing beans
Sowing time late spring (under glass) to early summer
Sowing or planting distance 15–25cm/6–10in
Sowing depth 4cm/1½in
Distance between sown rows 90cm/3ft
Thinning distance no need to thin
Harvesting late summer until first frosts

SOWING

Sow the beans in a single or double trench, once the threat of frosts has passed.

HARVESTING

Do not to pull too hard when harvesting French (green) beans because the plants may be pulled from the ground.

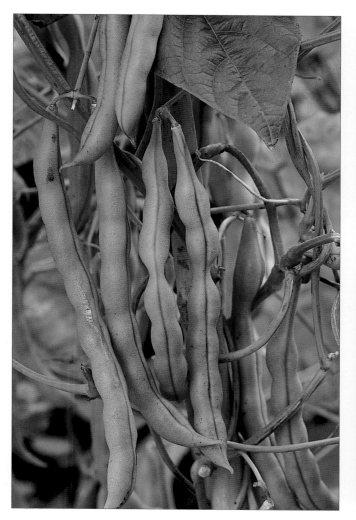

ABOVE **These climbing French (green) beans are being supported by a bamboo cane.**

ABOVE **These striking purple French (green) beans are now ready for harvesting. It seems a shame to pick such a decorative crop.**

Varieties

Dwarf beans

'Annabel' green, slim pods, stringless

'Canadian Wonder' green, flat pods

'Daisy' green, long pods, stringless

'Delinel' green, slim pods, stringless

'Golddukat' yellow waxpod, pencil pods

'Golden Sands' yellow waxpod, stringless

'Masai' green, very slim pods

'Mont d'Or' yellow waxpod

'Purple Queen' purple, round pods, stringless

'Purple Tepee' purple, round pods, stringless

'Radar' round pods, stringless

'Royalty' purple, stringless

'Sprite' green, round pods, stringless

'Tendergreen' green, pencil pods, stringless

'The Prince' green, flat pods, early

Haricot (navy) beans

'Brown Dutch'

'Chevrier Vert'

'Comtessa de Chambord'

Climbing beans

'Blue Lake' green, round pods, stringless, white seeded

'Hunter' flat pods, stringless

'Kentucky Blue' round pods

'Largo' round pods, stringless

'Mont d'Or' golden, slightly flat pods, near-black beans

'Veitch's Climbing' green, flat pods

yellow-coloured French (green) beans

climbing French (green) beans

purple-coloured French (green) beans

French (green) beans

Broad (Fava) Beans
Vicia faba

Unlike other forms of bean, broad (fava) beans can be an acquired taste; not every-body likes them. However, when they are cooked straight from the plant, home-grown beans have a flavour that is never found in bought ones, so if you have not enjoyed them in the past, grow some and try them again – you may be pleasantly surprised. These beans also have the advantage of being one of the first vegetables of the year to mature. While the other two main forms of garden bean come from the Americas, the broad (fava) bean is native to the Old World, probably originating in the Near East. Like the pea, it has been grown since Neolithic times, and, also like the pea, it can be eaten fresh or it can be dried and stored, which is a valuable attribute that has been appreciated right up to the advent of the freezer.

ABOVE **A row of healthy young beans at an early stage of their growth.**

Broad (fava) beans are categorized in various ways. Sometimes it is by length of pod. The long-pods have up to eight kidney-shaped beans in each pod, whereas the Windsors, the short-podded form, have only half that number of seeds, each of which is rounded. They can also be categorized by the colour of the seeds, which can be green, white (pale green, really) or mahogany-red; green seeds are better for freezing. They are also categorized as dwarf or tall forms, the former being better for the small garden. Finally, they can be divided into those that can be overwintered and those that are best sown in spring; this generally corresponds to the divisions between long-pods and Windsors, as the long-pods tend to be hardier.

PINCHING OUT

Pinching out the tops of the beans is a good practice because it discourages blackfly. The tops can then be boiled and eaten.

Cultivation

These beans need an open, sunny site, which is protected from strong winds, especially if you are growing overwintering types. A reasonably fertile soil is required, and this is best achieved by incorporating manure or compost during the autumn dig. Over-wintering varieties can be sown in late autumn. Other types should be sown in late winter or early spring. Although new varieties have extended the sowing season until early summer, most varieties need to be sown before the end of spring.

Sow in double rows in a shallow trench, 23cm/9in wide and 4cm/1½in deep. Alternatively, sow each seed individually with a dibber. In both cases, the seeds should be about 23cm/9in apart, and the rows should be 60cm/24in apart. Seeds can also be raised in pots or modules in late winter under glass and planted out in spring.

Taller varieties will need to be supported with string tied to canes that are set at intervals along each side of the double row. When the beans are in full flower, pinch out the tender top by 8cm/3in to reduce the chance of blackfly infestation and to make the pods fill out. Water during dry periods.

Harvesting

Pick the pods when the beans inside them have swollen. Some can be picked at an earlier stage for cooking whole. Do not allow the beans to become too old – that is, when they are leathery and pliable – or they will be tough and too floury. Some people like to cook and eat the young tops when they are removed.

Storage

These beans are undoubtedly best when picked straight from the plant, but any excess can be frozen for future use. They can also be dried.

Pests and diseases

The most serious problem is blackfly, but this can often be avoided by removing the tips of the plant (see left). On the whole, these beans are reasonably trouble free, although chocolate spot can be a problem. This can usually be ignored, but burn or destroy the affected plants when they are finished with rather than put them on the compost heap.

STAKING

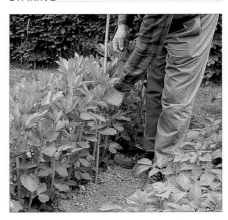

Taller varieties of broad (fava) beans will need supporting with string tied to canes that are set at intervals along the rows.

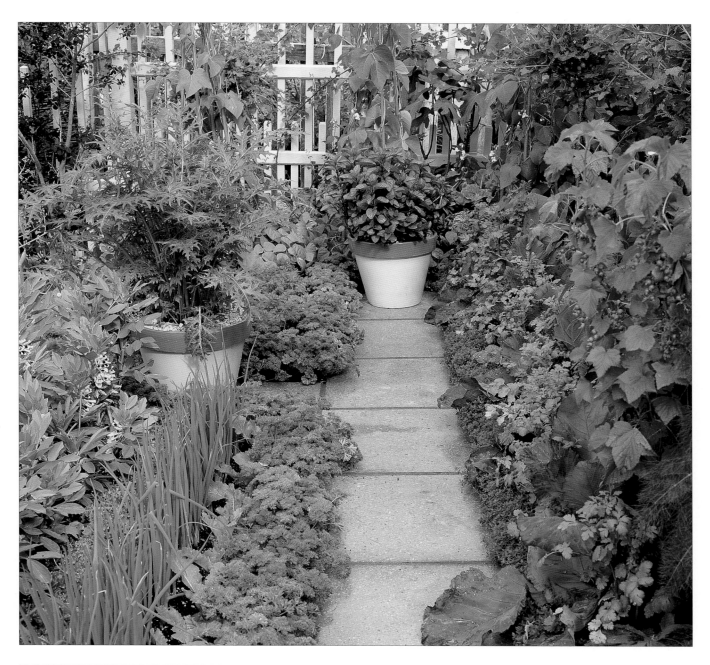

Varieties

'Aquadulce Claudia' long-pod, white seeds
'Bunyards Exhibition' long-pod, white seeds
'Express' pale green seeds
'Hylon' long-pod, white seeds
'Imperial Green Longpod' long-pod, green seeds
'Jade' long-pod, green
'Jubilee Hysor' white seeds

'Jumbo' large green seeds
'Masterpiece Green Longpod' long-pod, green seeds
'Meteor Vroma' green seeds
'Red Epicure' red seeds
'Relon' long-pod, green seeds
'The Sutton' dwarf, pale green seeds
'White Windsor' white seeds

broad (fava) beans

Cultivation

Sowing time late autumn, late winter to late spring
Sowing or planting distance 23cm/9in
Sowing depth 4cm/1½in
Distance between sown rows 60cm/24in
Thinning distance no need to thin
Harvesting early to late summer

MARROWS & SQUASH CROPS

Marrows and Courgettes (Zucchini)
Cucurbita pepo

Although marrows (zucchini), pumpkins and squashes are essentially the same plant, they are dealt with separately because they are usually considered differently in the garden and kitchen. First, it is important to consider the difference between marrows and courgettes (zucchini). In fact, there is no real difference: courgettes are an immature form of marrow, and, if left to grow, will turn into marrows. However, some varieties are best grown as one or the other.

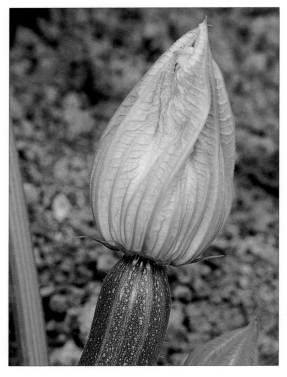

ABOVE **A female flower on a developing courgette (zucchini). The male flowers are often picked before they are open and used in cooking.**

The history of the marrow (zucchini) is not really known, and although they came to Europe from North America, there are no longer any native species that correspond to the plants we grow today. The marrow reached Europe in the 16th century and has been grown ever since. The idea of eating immature marrows as courgettes (zucchini) is a relatively recent development.

There are two types of marrows (zucchini): trailing and bush. The trailing forms throw out long stems that cover a great deal of space, and can be trained over a trellis or archway. The fruits appear at intervals along the stems. Bush varieties are much more compact, and the fruits grow from the central cluster of stems. They take up less space and are far better plants for small gardens. Courgettes (zucchini) are usually only grown as bushes; marrows are grown as either type.

In recent years courgettes (zucchini) have become much more popular than marrows (zucchini), partly because many people find that marrows are watery and bland and partly because, as families have become smaller, a whole marrow is difficult to dispose of in one sitting. However, marrows still have their devotees, and there are some very tasty ways of cooking them.

Courgettes (zucchini), on the other hand, are not only a more convenient size but, being immature, they do not dissolve into pulp quite so readily when they are cooked. They also have a more positive flavour. Nearly everybody who grows courgettes accidentally leaves at least one on the plant, which develops into a marrow (zucchini), so there is every opportunity of trying both. The flowers can also be eaten, either raw or cooked.

Marrows (zucchini) were traditionally grown on compost heaps. The heaps or bins were made up during winter and spring, topped with earth and left until the following autumn before being spread. The high

LEFT **Do not plant courgettes (zucchini) too close together; leave space to harvest the fruit.**

concentration of rich, fibrous material meant that moisture and nutrients were in abundant supply, creating the ideal conditions for these plants during the summer growing season. They can, of course, be grown in ordinary vegetable plots, but using the compost heap does save space, which can be used for other crops.

Cultivation
Marrows and courgettes (zucchini) like an open, sunny situation and a rich, moisture-retentive soil. As noted above, they can be grown on the compost heap or in a bed that has been heavily manured during the previous autumn. They are frost tender, so plants should not be put outside before the last frosts have passed, unless they are protected with cloches.

Plants can be raised under glass by sowing the flat seed edgeways in individual pots or in modules in late spring or sown directly in the

PLANTING OUT

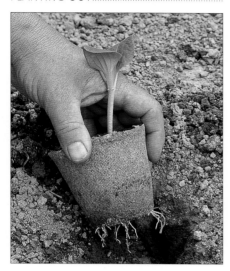

This marrow (zucchini) is being planted in its fibre pot. It has been grown like this to prevent disturbing the roots.

soil in early summer. Germination is speeded up by soaking the seed in water overnight. Keep seed that has been planted in the open warm by covering the soil with a jamjar or cloche until the seed has germinated. Sow two seeds at each position and remove the weaker if both germinate. Even if you sow in the open, sow a few in pots as insurance against sudden cold weather or the ravages of slugs.

Bush types can be left to develop by themselves but trailing varieties may need to be trimmed back if they get too vigorous. They can be left to trail outwards, like the spokes of a wheel, if there is enough space or they can be trained round in a circle, if

HARVESTING

Harvest a marrow (zucchini) by cutting it off at the base with a sharp knife.

Cultivation

Bush
Sowing time late spring (under glass) to early summer
Sowing or planting distance 90cm/3ft
Sowing depth 4cm/1½in
Distance between sown rows 90cm/3ft
Thinning distance no need to thin
Harvesting midsummer onwards

Trailing
Sowing time late spring (under glass) to early summer
Sowing or planting distance 1.2–1.8m/4–6ft
Sowing depth 4cm/1½in
Distance between sown rows 1.8m/6ft
Thinning distance no need to thin
Harvesting midsummer onwards

the stems are pegged down as they grow. If they are grown up a trellis or some other support, the shoots must be tied in regularly. Towards the end of summer remove the tips of each shoot. Keep well watered.

Harvesting

Courgettes (zucchini) are best harvested while they are still young – that is, when they are about 10cm/4in long – but in practice they can be harvested at any time, and circumstances usually dictate that they are picked at any stage between being a courgette and a small marrow (zucchini). If they are left on the plant, courgettes will eventually develop into full marrows and can be cut at any time until the first frosts. Whatever the size of the crop, cut through the stem 2cm/¾in or more away from the fruit.

Storage

Courgettes (zucchini) are difficult to store for more than a few days and are best eaten fresh from the plant. They can be frozen, although they become less firm. Marrows (zucchini), in contrast, will last for several weeks after picking, especially if they have been left to mature and ripen. Pick marrows at the end of the season, before the first frosts, and then store them in a frost-free place for several weeks, on trays or hanging in net bags.

Pests and diseases

Although generally trouble free, slugs are the most severe problem, eating right through the stem if not checked.

Cucumber mosaic virus is the most common disease, causing mottled leaves and distorted fruit. The plant should be burned or destroyed. In some years powdery mildew is also a problem; rightly or wrongly gardeners tend to ignore it.

Varieties

Bush	Trailing	Courgettes (Zucchini)
'All Green Bush'	'Long Green Trailing'	'Ambassador'
'Badger Cross'	'Long White Trailing'	'Burpee Golden Zucchini'
'Green Bush'	'Table Dainty'	'Bush Champion'
'Long Green Bush'	'Tender and True'	'Defender'
'Long White Bush'		'Early Gem'
'Minipak'		'Gold Rush'
		'Greyzini'
		'Tondo di Nizza'
		'Zucchini'

marrows (zucchini)

courgettes (zucchini)

Cucumbers

Cucumis sativus

One of the quickest ways to prepare a meal is to pop into the garden, grab a lettuce, some tomatoes and a cucumber. Add some fresh, crusty bread – and there you are. Most gardeners grow lettuces and tomatoes, but fewer grow cucumbers, perhaps because they think they require a greenhouse or they are difficult to grow. They need not be either. Outdoor cucumbers can be grown as easily as courgettes (zucchini), which few gardeners find a problem.

Cucumbers have been used as a vegetable for the best part of 5,000 years. They were first grown and eaten in India, where they were developed from a native species, and from there they spread north-east into China and north-west into Greece and Rome.

There are several colours and shapes. In the West we are more used to long cucumbers with green skins, but they can also be oval or even round, and colours can range from white to yellow.

As far as the gardener is concerned, there are two types of cucumber: the climbing varieties with long fruit that are grown under glass and the ridge varieties that are much shorter and are grown in the open. The advantage of greenhouse varieties is that they can be started earlier and are not as dependent on the weather. Ridge varieties, on the other hand, need less looking after and are less prone to attack by pests and diseases, which thrive in the warmth of the greenhouse. From the culinary point of view, the greenhouse forms are often preferred, mainly because outdoor cucumbers have tough, often prickly, skins and do not look quite as elegant as their indoor cousins. Until recently, many outdoor varieties tended to taste bitter, but this is now no longer generally the case.

Gherkins are a form of ridge cucumber, which are used for pickling. Any immature ridge cucumber can be used, but some varieties have been specially bred for the purpose. Like courgettes and marrows (zucchini), there is no difference in cultivation technique other than the time of picking.

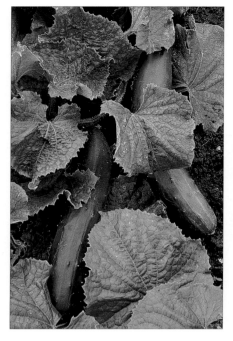

ABOVE **Ridge or outdoor cucumbers growing in the open need a sunny spot that is sheltered from the wind.**

Cultivation

Greenhouse cucumbers need a high temperature in which to germinate and a high temperature in which to grow. Using seed of all-female varieties – they are less likely to be bitter – sow two seeds, edgeways, in pots or modules and place in a propagator at 24°C/75°F. When they germinate, remove the weaker seedling and reduce the temperature to 21°C/70°F. Plant the young plants with as little root disturbance as possible into growing bags, two per bag depending on the size. Use square-meshed netting or a system of poles and horizontal wires as supports, and tie in the shoots as they grow. Pinch out the tip of the shoot when it reaches the roof. Tie the laterals to horizontal wires and pinch out the tips two leaves beyond the first fruit to form. Water to keep the soil constantly moist and throw some water on the floor of the greenhouse to keep the atmosphere humid. Keep the house shaded. Once the fruit start to develop, feed them with a high-potash liquid feed once every two weeks.

Ridge or outdoor cucumbers need a sunny spot sheltered from the wind. Add plenty of well-rotted manure to the soil before sowing. Sow ridge cucumbers either inside in pots or outdoors where they are to grow. If sown directly, cover them with a glass jamjar or cloche to raise the temperature. Do not sow until after the threat of frost has passed and the soil has warmed up. Sow, leaving about 75cm/30in in each direction between plants. If the seed is germinated in pots, ensure that the roots are not disturbed when they are transplanted. Fibre pots can help with this,

LEFT **A ridge or outdoor cucumber, with its attractive yellow flowers and tough, prickly skin clearly on display.**

Cultivation

Greenhouse
Sowing time late winter onwards
Sowing or planting distance 60cm/24in
Sowing depth 2.5cm/1in
Thinning distance no need to thin
Harvesting midsummer onwards
Ridge
Sowing time late spring (under glass)
to early summer
Sowing or planting distance 75cm/30in
Sowing depth 2.5cm/1in
Distance between sown rows 75cm/30in
Thinning distance no need to thin
Harvesting midsummer onwards

ABOVE **This ridge or outdoor cucumber has been trained up a cane tripod. The large leaves and fruits have a pleasing architectural quality.**

because the cucumbers can be planted without removing them from the pots. Pinch out the tip of the main shoot after six leaves have formed so that the plant bushes out. Water freely. Once the fruit start to develop, feed with a high-potash liquid feed once every two weeks.

Harvesting
Cut the fruit with a short length of stalk as soon as they are large enough to eat. Pick frequently and more fruit will develop. Harvest gherkins when they are 5–8cm/ 2–3in long.

Varieties

Ridge	'Pepinex'
'Burpless Tasty Green'	'Petita'
'Bush Champion'	'Telegraph'
'Crystal Apple'	'Telegraph'
'Long Green Ridge'	Improved'
'Masterpiece'	**Gherkins**
Greenhouse	'Bestal'
'Birgit'	'Venlo'
'Fenumex'	Pickling'

Storage
Keep for no more more than a few days; they are best eaten fresh.

Pests and diseases
Slugs and snails can quickly eat through a stem, killing the plant; remove by your preferred method. In the greenhouse, red spider mite and whitefly may be a problem.

ABOVE **Climbing varieties of cucumber are grown under glass. They have smooth skins and are longer than ridge varieties.**

ridge cucumber

greenhouse cucumber

SHOOT CROPS

Asparagus
Asparagus officinalis

Asparagus was once the food of the wealthy – if you didn't have your own garden, you couldn't grow it. Nowadays it is much more widely available, but shoots cut straight from the garden and cooked immediately still taste best. Asparagus is not only good to eat, but the decorative foliage has a wonderful filmy quality about it. A great uncle of mine grew asparagus all his long life, not to eat it, but so that he could use the cut foliage with his sweet peas. In a potager or decorative kitchen garden, the great plumes of finely cut foliage make a fine display.

ABOVE **Harvest asparagus by cutting the stems below the ground.**

The tender shoot of asparagus is the part of the plant that is eaten. The shoot emerges from below ground in late spring and early summer. Once it gets above approximately 15–20cm/6–8in long it becomes tough-skinned and rather chewy and is then best left, the remaining shoots developing into tall foliage stems with inconspicuous flowers and, eventually, orange-red berries.

Asparagus grows wild throughout Europe and has been eaten and possibly cultivated from at least the time of the Ancient Greeks. It has long been grown in gardens, but the main disadvantage is that it takes up quite a lot of space. If you have a small garden but want to grow asparagus, try planting one or two crowns in the flower borders, picking the spikes in early summer and then leaving them in the border as a decorative foliage plant.

One of the attractive features of creating an asparagus bed is that it lasts for at least 20 years, and apart from a little maintenance, not much effort is required to produce a wonderful feast each year. Asparagus plants are either male or female. Male plants have the advantage of being more productive and not producing seed (which readily self-sows). Asparagus can be raised from seed, but the results can be disappointing if you use your own collected seed; it is better to buy named varieties on which you can rely. An increasing number of F1 hybrids is available, and these produce very good all-male plants.

Cultivation

Asparagus needs an open, sunny site, and it likes a light, preferably sandy soil, although it can be grown in any soil as long as it is free-draining and reasonably fertile. In heavy soils it can be grown by raising the level of the soil or by making a raised bed. In the autumn before planting, dig the bed, removing all traces of perennial weeds and incorporating plenty of well-rotted manure or compost. In the spring dig out a trench 20cm/8in deep with an 8cm/3in ridge running down the centre. If more than one row is required, set the trenches 90cm/3ft apart. Set each asparagus crown on the ridge, spreading out its roots around it.

Each crown should be 45cm/18in apart. Cover them with soil to a depth of 8–10cm/3–4in.

If you are growing from seed, soak them overnight in water and sow in a drill 1cm/½in deep. Do this in spring. Thin to 15cm/6in and transplant the following spring in the same manner as for bought crowns above. As the plants grow, draw in more earth from the side of the trench until it is filled.

Do not cut any spears in the first year and only one or two from each plant during the next year. Each spring, cover the trench with a layer of manure or compost, leaving it slightly heaped up so that over the years the row becomes earthed (hilled) up in the

APPLYING A SPRING MULCH

In the spring, before growth starts, apply a deep mulch of manure over the rows of asparagus.

CUTTING DOWN IN AUTUMN

In the autumn, as the asparagus fronds are turning brown, cut them down to the ground.

same way you treat potatoes. Keep the ground weeded. Cut down the ferns as they begin to turn yellow and, if possible, before the berries begin to ripen; alternatively, pick all the berries. If they are left on the plants the birds will eat them and before long asparagus will be appearing all over the garden. For the same reason, avoid putting berried stems on the compost heap.

Harvesting

In late spring, when the shoots that have emerged are 10–15cm/4–6in long, cut them by inserting a knife 5cm/2in below the surface of the soil. Only cut through the stem, do not thrash around below the soil level or you may damage spears that have not yet emerged. Make a slanting cut. After the third year cutting can take place over about six weeks.

Storage

Asparagus is best used fresh from the plant, but it can be stored for a couple of days if it is stood in a jug of cold water in the refrigerator.

ABOVE **Once the harvesting season is over, the asparagus is left to grow to its full height.**

Pests and diseases

Asparagus is usually pest and disease free. Slugs, as usual, are likely to be the worst problem, making holes in the spears. Asparagus beetle can also be a nuisance.

asparagus

Cultivation
Sowing
Sowing time spring
Sowing depth 1cm/½in
Distance between sown rows 30cm/12in
Thinning distance 15cm/6in
Transplanting following spring
Planting
Planting time early spring
Planting distance 45cm/18in
Planting depth initially 8–10cm/3–4in
Distance between sown rows 90cm/3ft
Harvesting in late spring for six weeks
(third year onwards)

Varieties	
'Accell'	'Giant Mammoth'
'Boonlim'	'Limbras'
'Cito'	'Lucullus'
'Connover's Colossal'	'Martha
'Franklin'	Washington'

Celery

Apium graveolens

Celery is an important vegetable for the kitchen as it is used, at least in part, in many dishes, including basic recipes such as stocks. Its culinary importance is not reflected in the garden, however. At one time no vegetable garden was complete without celery, but it is seen less often today, which may be partly because it is slightly difficult to grow and partly because it needs a constantly moist soil to do well. Whatever the reason, it is a shame it is not more widely grown, because if you do grow it you will find that you are constantly using it and, as always, will find the flavour so much better than shop-bought stalks.

Celery grows wild throughout Europe and Asia, and it is rather surprising to learn that it has entered cultivation only in relatively recent times. Celery was first cultivated in Italy as recently as the 16th century but it did not arrive in Britain until the end of the 17th century.

It is the blanched leaf stalks of celery that are eaten. These can be eaten green but taste sweeter if the light has been excluded, causing the stalks to turn white. This always used to be done by heaping earth up round them, but more often these days the stems are wrapped in cardboard or felt. This type of celery is often referred to as trench celery. Breeding has produced celery with self-blanching stems, although not everybody feels that these are wholly successful and that the old-style blanched stalks taste better. There are also forms with green, pink or red stems. There is a form of celery, known as green or American celery, which does not require blanching.

As well as the stems, some people like to eat the heart, the solid part of the plant, where the stems join the root. Some recipes also call for the leaves to be included, particularly when the celery is a flavouring agent rather than a vegetable in its own right. It can be cooked or eaten raw.

Cultivation

There are two ways of growing celery, depending on what type is being grown. To grow traditional trench celery, in the preceding autumn or winter dig out a trench 45cm/18in wide and 30cm/12in deep and put in an 8cm/3in layer of rotted manure. Backfill the trench, leaving it about 10cm/4in deep. Sow the seeds under glass in modules in early spring and place them in moderate heat of 10–16°C/50–61°F. Do not check the

ABOVE **Green varieties of celery, such as the one shown here, do not need blanching.**

plants by subjecting them to a sudden change of temperature or by allowing them to dry out. Once the frosts are over, harden off the plants and plant them out in the trench at 30cm/12in intervals. When the plants reach about 30cm/12in, tie the stems loosely together just below the leaves and draw up earth over part of the stems. Repeat the process three weeks later, pulling up more soil, and again three weeks after this, until the soil is up to the lower leaves. Alternatively,

BLANCHING CELERY

1 Blanching celery stems will make them taste sweeter. When the stems reach a height of about 30cm/12in, tie them loosely together just below the leaves.

2 A collar of cardboard or waterproof paper is tied around the stems of celery. The stems eventually blanch because of the lack of light.

3 Soil can be used to hold the collar in place. Although soil can also be earthed up around the stems to blanch them, a collar will stop soil from getting into the crown.

ABOVE **The celery planted here with some cabbages is one of the self-blanching varieties now available – 'Golden Self-blanching'.**

plant on flat ground and wrap cardboard or waterproof paper round the stems when they are 30cm/12in long. When the stems grow taller, wrap a second collar round them. Keep the celery well watered and do not allow the soil to dry out.

Self-blanching celery is started in the same way from seed and then planted out in blocks rather than rows, setting the plants at intervals of 23cm/9in in all directions. The dense foliage helps to blanch the stems. Place straw around the outside of the block to help keep out the light. Green celery can be grown in the same way, although there is no need for the straw.

HARVESTING

Harvest the celery by digging beneath it with a fork and levering it out of the soil. Replace any soil around the next plant if it falls away.

ABOVE **The celery planted here with some cabbages is one of the self-blanching varieties now available – 'Golden Self-blanching'.**

Harvesting

Trench celery can be lifted in autumn by digging it up with a fork. Replace soil around the next plant if it falls away. Continue to dig as required. The flavour is improved by the first frosts, but cover the plants with straw in severe weather so that penetrating frosts do not reach the stems. Self-blanching celery can also be harvested as required from the autumn onwards, but it should be lifted by the time of the first winter frosts.

Storage

Leave trench varieties where they are growing until required. In colder areas, before the weather becomes severe, lift and store in a frost-free place, where they should stay fresh for several weeks. Celery can be frozen, but it becomes mushy when it is defrosted, so it can only be used as flavouring or in cooked dishes.

Pests and diseases

Slugs are one of the worst enemies of celery, and it is important to cull them regularly by your preferred method. Other problems can include celery fly and carrot fly.

Diseases include celery heart rot and celery leaf spot. Boron deficiency, which causes the stems to crack, may also be a problem.

Cultivation	
Trench	
Sowing time early to mid-spring	
Planting date early summer	
Planting distance 30cm/12in	
Distance between sown rows 60cm/24in	
Harvesting autumn onwards	
Self-blanching	
Sowing time early to mid-spring	
Planting date early summer	
Planting distance in blocks 23cm/9in	
Harvesting autumn	

Varieties	
Trench	'Golden Self-blanching'
'Giant Pink'	'Ivory Tower'
'Giant Red'	'Lathom's
'Giant White'	Self-blanching'
'Hopkins Fenlander'	'Victoria'
'Martine'	**Green**
'New White Dwarf'	'Greensnap'
Self-blanching	'Imperial'
'Celebrity'	'Tall Utah'

trench celery

Rhubarb
Rheum × hybridum

Gardening has many contradictions and rhubarb is one of them. It is a vegetable, but it is mainly used as a fruit – that is, it is eaten with sugar as a dessert. Tomatoes, on the other hand, are, strictly speaking, fruit but are used as a vegetable. Does it matter? These are problems only when you start classifying plants or writing books; in the garden and kitchen it doesn't matter at all.

Originally rhubarb was grown as a medicinal plant (the root was powdered and used as a laxative), and it was only much later that it was used as a vegetable. It was used in medicine nearly 5,000 years ago in Ancient China, but it was only in the 18th century that it was realized that it also made a good vegetable. Forcing to obtain an early crop was not discovered (accidentally, as all good discoveries seem to be) until early in the following century, less than 200 years ago.

Only the young stalks are eaten, and these must be cooked. The leaves are

Cultivation
Seed
Sowing time spring
Sowing depth 2.5cm/1in
Distance between sown rows 30cm/12in
Thinning distance 23cm/9in
Transplanting following winter
Division
Planting time winter or (if potted) spring
Planting distance 90cm/3ft
Distance between rows 90cm/3ft
Harvesting summer of second year onwards

poisonous, so do not be tempted to experiment with them in an attempt to invent new dishes. The crop is normally harvested from spring to early summer, but it is possible to "force" it, by covering the dormant crown with a box, bucket or, if you can afford it, a decorative terracotta rhubarb forcer. This produces a crop of sweet-tasting stems, several weeks earlier than if the plant is left in the open.

Rhubarb is an easy crop to grow and, once planted, it is not at all demanding. It can be left where it is for 20 years or more, although some gardeners prefer to replace their plants every five years or so in order to keep them vigorous. Rhubarb does take up quite a bit of space, but a couple of plants will keep a small family well supplied. The space may be considered well used because rhubarb plants are also quite decorative, with their huge green leaves and attractive red stems. In summer they throw up large flowering stems, covered with masses of creamy flowers, which can be spectacular.

Cultivation

Rhubarb must have a sunny position, away from shade. The soil should be rich in organic material but it should also be reasonably free draining. Because the site will be in use over a long period of time, take care in its preparation, removing all perennial weeds and digging deeply to incorporate as much well-rotted manure as

LEFT **A decorative terracotta rhubarb forcer for producing sweet early rhubarb. Alternatively, a box or bucket can be used.**

possible. In the past new plants were bare rooted and were planted in winter, while they were dormant. This is also a good time to divide an existing plant to start a new one: dig up the old plant and remove an outer section that includes at least one bud. Plants that are purchased in pots can be planted in spring or even summer if they are kept well-watered. They should be spaced 90cm/3ft apart.

Rhubarb can also be grown from seed, but this method takes longer and the quality of the plant cannot be guaranteed in the same way as buying a named cultivar. However, the seed can be sown in 2.5cm/1in drills and thinned to 23cm/9in once they have germinated. Plant out in their final position, in the same way as for dormant crowns, during the following winter. Water well in dry weather. Apply a mulch of well-rotted, seed-free manure in autumn and again in spring.

To force a rhubarb plant, cover it with a large upturned bucket or other similar container in midwinter. Do not force the same plant for two years running or it will be weakened.

HARVESTING

Harvest by pulling on the sticks of rhubarb so that they come out of their "socket". Cut off the leaves and discard on the compost heap.

ABOVE **A bed of healthy looking rhubarb is an attractive sight. Remember that rhubarb leaves are poisonous and cannot be eaten.**

rhubarb

Harvesting

Rhubarb is harvested from spring to early summer unless it has been forced, when it can be pulled a few weeks earlier. It is harvested by pulling each stem vertically from close to the base – it will come out of its "socket". Cut off the leaves and discard on the compost heap.

Storage

Rhubarb is best cooked straight from the garden. Otherwise it can be stored by freezing or bottling.

Pests and diseases

There are a few pests and diseases that trouble rhubarb, but you will be unfortunate if you come across them.

Varieties	
'Appleton's Forcing'	'Hawkes Champagne'
'Canada Red'	'Macdonald'
'Champagne'	'The Sutton'
'Early Victoria'	'Timperley Early'
'Glaskin's Perpetual'	'Victoria'

FRUITING VEGETABLES

Aubergines (Eggplants)
Solanum melongena

Surprisingly the aubergine (eggplant) is related to the potato although so different. Now popular vegetables in the shops, aubergines have never really been widely grown in the garden and the young plants especially need shelter and warmth. Things are changing, however, and more gardeners are attempting to grow these attractive fruits.

The aubergine (eggplant) is a tropical plant, coming mainly from India where it was grown over 2,000 years ago. Introduced into southern Europe, in particular Spain, in the 16th century by the Arabs, it subsequently became popular throughout the countries bordering the Mediterranean, especially Greece.

The plants grow to about 45cm/18in tall, although they will be taller under glass, and they have soft, felted leaves. Some forms retain prickly fruit stems, but this characteristic has been bred out of some of the more modern cultivars. The fruits that we usually see in shops are long and a deep, shiny purple, sometimes almost black, but those that are grown from seed can be a variety of colours. The alternative name, eggplant, derives from those forms that produce round, white, egg-shaped fruit – there is even a variety called 'Easter Egg'. Other varieties bear fruits that are striped in white and purple or white and mauve. The shapes of the fruits also vary considerably, from almost round to long and thin, and these look like a cross between a bean and a chilli pepper (to which they are, in fact, related). The variation is such that the aubergine has become something of a cult with a number of growers in much the same way that pumpkins and squashes are with others. It is easy to see why.

The aubergine (eggplant) can be cooked as a vegetable by itself or it can be combined with other ingredients in more complicated dishes. Increasing interest in Mediterranean cooking has also stimulated interest in growing these plants, and there is now good reason to grow them as a vegetable rather than just as a curiosity.

Because of its tropical origins, aubergine (eggplant) is best grown under glass unless a favoured sunny spot can be found. This is, perhaps, one reason why it has not hitherto been popular, as most greenhouses are taken up with tomatoes and cucumbers.

Cultivation

Aubergines (eggplants) need a warm, sunny position, which is usually best provided in a greenhouse. Even where they can be grown outside, they need to be started off inside. Soak the seeds in water overnight before sowing, then sow in spring in modules or individual pots. The seeds will germinate in a temperature of 21–25°C/70–77°F. If seed is sown in trays, prick out the seedlings as

ABOVE **This swelling fruit shows the glorious purple colour of the most common aubergines (egglants).**

soon as they are large enough to handle. Once they are big enough they can be planted out into growing bags (two to a bag) or into large pots in the greenhouse. If the temperature does not drop below 15°C/59°F, after hardening off they can be planted outside or moved in the pots to a sheltered position outside. The best results, however, are usually obtained by growing under glass.

Use canes or strings to support the growing plants once they get above 45–60cm/18–24in. Pinch out the tips of the plants when they reach about 38cm/15in high to encourage the formation of fruit. Keep the plants well watered, and feed once every ten days with a high-potash liquid feed once the fruit has started to develop.

Harvesting

The fruits can be picked as soon as they are large enough, which should be from midsummer onwards in a greenhouse, but from

PLANTING IN CONTAINERS

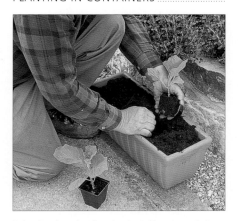

Aubergines (eggplants) can be planted in pots or window boxes and moved outside when the weather is warmer.

autumn outside. Cut each one with a piece of stalk on it, and remember that those that have lost their shine taste bitter and are not worth eating.

Storage

Aubergines (eggplants) are best eaten fresh from the plant, straight from the garden,

although they can be kept for up to two weeks before use in the kitchen.

Pests and diseases

The pests that are most likely to cause trouble are the normal greenhouse ones, such as aphids, red spider mite and whitefly. Dampen the floor of the house and spray the plants with water to maintain humid conditions to discourage red spider mite.

ABOVE **In warm areas, aubergines (eggplants) can be planted directly in the soil in the open garden.**

aubergines

Cultivation
Sowing time spring
Sowing in modules or pots
Planting time inside mid-spring
Planting time outside early summer
Planting distance 50cm/20in
Distance between sown rows 50cm/20in
Harvesting midsummer onwards

Varieties	
'Black Beauty'	'Easter Egg'
'Black Bell'	'Long Purple'
'Black Enorma'	'Moneymaker'
'Black Prince'	'Short Tom'
'Bonica'	'Slice Rite'

Peppers

Capsicum species

Increasing interest in Mediterranean cooking has been accompanied by an increase in the popularity of peppers, of which the main type are the sweet peppers or bell peppers (Capsicum annuum Grossum Group). These are the large green, red and yellow fruits we see in supermarkets – the green peppers are, in fact, the unripe versions of the red and yellow fruit. They can be used raw or cooked, usually with all the seeds removed. The plants are bushy in habit, growing up to 75cm/30in in good conditions.

The chillies (*Capsicum annuum* Longum Group) are also a fairly recent crop for most gardeners, again stimulated by changes in eating habits, although they were probably the first types to be grown in Europe. The fruits, usually red in colour, are long and pointed. They are hot to the taste, becoming hotter as the fruit matures. It is the seed and the pith that are the main hot ingredients, and if these are removed, the fruit can be made milder. Chillies are often dried.

Finally, there are the hot or cayenne peppers or tabasco, which belong to a different species, *Capsicum frutescens*. These are smaller than chilli peppers and are generally even hotter. The narrow fruits, which can be yellow, orange or red in colour, are often used dried. They are the most difficult and less usual of the peppers to grow.

Peppers originated in Mexico and Central America, and they were thus a relatively late introduction to Europe – sometime late in the 15th or early 16th century. They have, however, been cultivated in their native lands for at least 7,000 years and perhaps much longer. Once in Europe, they were adopted far more readily in the Mediterranean countries, where they are still used more than in northern Europe.

Cultivation

Sowing time spring
Sowing in modules or pots
Planting time inside mid-spring
Planting time outside early summer
Planting distance 50cm/20in
Distance between sown rows 50cm/20in
Harvesting midsummer onwards

Peppers can be grown outside in warmer districts, but generally they do best under glass. If they are grown outside, the best method is to grow them in containers or growing bags, in a warm, sheltered position, against a south-facing wall. In warmer areas they can be grown in a border.

Cultivation

Seed should be sown in spring in a propagator, set at about 18°C/65°F. They can be sown in modules, individual pots or trays. If trays are used, prick out the resulting seedlings as soon as they are large enough to handle. As soon as they are big enough they can be transferred to growing bags (two or three to a bag) or into large pots. The advantage of pots is that they can easily be moved outside if the weather is warm enough. Pinch out the tops of the young plants when they get to 15–20cm/ 6–8in to make them bush out. If the bushes get above 45–50cm/18–20in they may need to be supported with canes or strings. If they are grown in an outside bed, plant them out in early summer when the temperature has warmed up and set them at 50cm/20in intervals in a fertile, but free-draining soil. Keep the peppers well watered and feed every ten days with a high-potash liquid feed once the fruits start to swell.

Harvesting

Start picking in mid- to late summer when the fruits are large enough – for peppers this is usually when they are about the size of a tennis ball. They can be harvested when they are green or have changed to

LEFT **Green peppers are the unripe fruit, yellow peppers are the first stage in the ripening process, and red peppers are the final stage.**

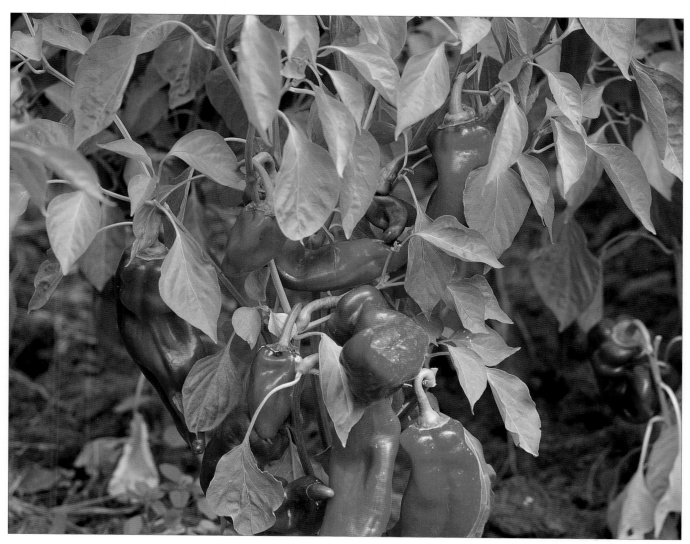

ABOVE **Not all peppers are the evenly shaped fruit that we find in our supermarkets.**

their final red or yellow coloration. Some cultivars are best picked green. The hot or cayenne peppers should be fully ripe and coloured before they are picked. Cut the fruit so that about 2.5cm/1in of stalk is left.

Storage

Sweet peppers are best eaten straight from the plant, but they can be kept for up to two weeks before being used. Other types of pepper can be dried.

Pests and diseases

The pests that are most likely to cause trouble are the usual greenhouse ones such as aphids, red spider mite and whitefly. Dampen the floor of the house and spray the plants with water to maintain humid conditions to discourage red spider mite. Both inside and outside the greenhouse, however, the major problem is likely to be aphids on the young shoots.

Varieties	
Sweet peppers	**Chilli peppers**
'Ace'	Sometime listed
'Antaro'	simply as chillies.
'Ariane'	'Apache''
'Bell Boy'	'De Fresno Chilli
'Bendigo'	Grande'
'California Wonder'	'Hot Gold Spike'
'Canape'	'Hot Mexican'
'Clio'	'Red Chilli'
'Delphin'	'Serrano Chilli'
'Gypsy'	**Cayenne**
'Hungarian Wax'	**peppers**
'Luteus'	Often listed simply as
'Marconi'	cayenne.
'New Ace'	'Cayenne Large Red'
'Redskin'	'Cayenne Long Slim'
'Sweet Spanish	'Red Cherry Small'
Mixed'	'Super Cayenne'
'Yellow Lantern'	'Tabasco'

sweet peppers

chilli peppers

Sweet Corn (Corn)

Zea mays

Sweet corn, maize or corn-on-the-cob (Zea mays) is a cereal. It is a rather dramatic plant, growing up to 1.5m/5ft or more. The airy spikes of male flowers decorate the top of the plant, and the cobs, with their female flowers, form where the broad strap-like leaves join the main stem. They have an ornamental quality that makes them worth growing in the decorative kitchen garden.

Although maize has a long history, going back to prehistoric times, it is a relatively recent introduction to Europe. This is because it comes from Mexico and it was only after the Spanish Conquest in the early 16th century that it was brought to the Old World. In Europe the main varieties are yellow or yellow and white, but in the Americas, where it has had such a long tradition, there are many more varieties, often with quite deeply coloured seeds, including black.

Because of its size, sweet corn (corn) takes up a lot of space in the garden, but the superior taste of fresh sweet corn, compared with corn bought in the shops,

which may be days old, makes it worth trying to find the space, even if it is only for a few plants. Sweet corn needs to be grown in a block rather than in rows, which increases the chances of pollen falling from the higher male flowers onto the female ones below. This may be inconvenient in terms of the shape of your vegetable garden, but it is worth making the effort to find room.

Sweet corn (corn) needs as long a growing season as possible, but it is, unfortunately, frost tender, so the plants have to be started off under glass and transferred to open ground only when there is no further danger of frost. Seed can be sown directly into the soil, but this may not give a long enough

ABOVE **The dying tassel of a female flower hangs from the developing cob. This is an indication that the cob is ready for harvesting. Twist the cobs so that they snap off from the stem.**

season in some regions. Seed often carries a powdery fungicide to stop it from rotting in wet soils.

Cultivation

Sweet corn (corn) needs a warm, sunny position, sheltered from strong winds. The soil should be free draining and well prepared with rotted organic material. Sow the seeds in individual pots under glass in mid-spring, and germinate under gentle heat of 13–15°C/ 55–59°F. Harden off the plants before planting out in early summer or whenever there is no likelihood of frost. Plant in a block and set 30cm/12in apart.

Seed sown outside should be sown in late spring and protected by cloches. Sow two seeds together at 30cm/12in intervals in a block rather than a row. After germination remove the weaker seedling.

Once established, growing plants should have earth drawn up around the stems for about 15cm/6in or more to support them against wind in exposed areas. Avoid deep hoeing – this can disturb the shallow roots.

LEFT **These young sweet corn (corn) plants have been grown from seed under glass and then planted out in a block.**

Cultivation

Sowing time inside mid-spring
Sowing time outside early summer
Sowing inside in modules or pots
Planting-out time early summer
Planting and sowing distance
30cm/12in
Distance between sown rows 30cm/12in
Harvesting autumn

Varieties

'Butterscotch'	'Morning Sun'
'Dawn'	'Northern Belle'
'Dynasty'	'Pilot'
'Earliking'	'Sundance'
'Fiesta'	'Sunrise'
'Honeycomb'	'Sugar Boy'
'Kelvedon Glory'	'Sweet 77'
'Miracle'	'Yukon'

LEFT **These maturing sweet corn (corn) plants clearly show the spiky male flowers which are situated higher up than the female flowers.**

mature
sweet corn (corn)

immature sweet corn
(corn)

Harvesting

Harvest sweet corn (corn) when the tassels on the cobs begin to turn brown. Twist the cobs so that they snap off from the stem.

Storage

Sweet corn (corn) is best when cooked and eaten straight from the plant, although the cobs will keep a few days after they have been harvested. Cobs can also be frozen and then kept for winter use.

Pests and diseases

The main problem with sweet corn (corn) comes from mice and birds, which steal the seed. Frit fly and corn smut are the only other likely troubles, but fortunately they are not common.

Tomatoes

Lycopersicon esculentum

Tomatoes are probably the most widely grown of all vegetables. Even people without a garden often manage to grow a plant or two on a balcony or patio. One reason for this is that tomatoes are relatively easy to grow, but another must surely be that supermarket-bought tomatoes bear little resemblance to what a gardener knows as a tomato – there is very little relationship between the two flavours. Another reason may well be the sheer range of tomatoes that you can now grow. They come in all manner of tastes, sizes and colours, and even some of the old-fashioned varieties that have the best flavours are becoming more readily available. The largest, such as the beefsteak tomatoes, can weigh up to 450g/1lb each, while the smallest are not much more than the size of grapes.

ABOVE **Cordon tomatoes should be well supported. These special spirals support the plant without the necessity of tying them**.

Tomatoes can either be grown on cordons (upright plants) or as bushes. It is well worth not only growing your own particular favourite varieties each year, but also experimenting with at least one new one. This may well result in a glut of tomatoes, but they are wonderful things to give away.

Tomatoes are a very close relation to the potato. (If you want to try your skill at grafting, graft a young tomato plant onto one of the stems of a potato plant; it is actually possible to get potatoes underground and tomatoes above.) Like the potato, the tomato comes from South America, where it had probably been grown for centuries before it was bought to Europe in the 16th century. Because they belong to the family Solanaceae, of which deadly nightshade is also a member, they were at first treated with suspicion in Europe and used as ornamental plants. However, once they were accepted, it was the Mediterranean countries that used them most often in their cuisine. They do, of course, make very decorative plants, with their red, yellow or green fruits, and they are a valuable addition to potagers and other ornamental gardens.

Tomatoes are used widely both in raw and cooked dishes. They can even be used in their unripened state, so that any that have not ripened by the time the frosts arrive can still be used.

Tomatoes are half-hardy and can be grown under glass or outside. Earlier and later crops, as well as heavier ones, are obtained under glass, but outside crops often taste better, particularly if the summer has been hot and the fruit has ripened well.

Cultivation

If you are growing under glass, sow the seed in mid-spring in a very gentle heat or an unheated greenhouse. An earlier start can be made in a heated greenhouse to obtain earlier crops. As soon as they are big enough to handle, prick out the seedlings into individual pots. When the plants are large enough, transfer them to growing bags, large pots or a greenhouse border.

LEFT **A bed of tomato plants with good exposure to the sun for ripening.**

USING GROWING BAGS

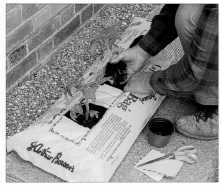

Tomatoes can be grown in bags of compost (soil mix).

PINCHING OUT SIDE SHOOTS

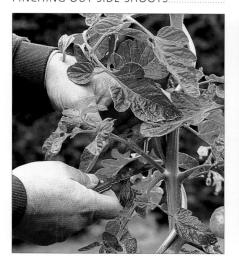

The side shoots on cordon varieties should be pinched or cut out.

HARVESTING

Harvest tomatoes when they are ripe, which will usually be when they turn red. Leave the stalk on.

RIPENING TOMATOES

At the end of the season, dig up any remaining plants and hang them upside down under protection to ripen.

(The soil will need changing, preferably every year, if tomatoes are planted directly into a border.) Arrange some form of support, such as strings or canes, for the tomatoes to be tied to as they grow. Remove any side shoots as they appear. Keep well watered and feed every ten days with a high-potash liquid fertilizer once the fruits begin to swell. Pinch out the top of the plant when it reaches the glass.

For cordons grown outdoors, the same procedure as above is followed, except that the plants are hardened off before being planted out, which should not be until after the last of the frosts. They should be in an open, sunny position and a fertile soil. Bush forms are treated in the same way, except that there is no need to remove the side shoots. They will also benefit from a straw mulch to keep the fruit off the soil. The end of the season usually comes before all the fruit has ripened. Either use them in recipes that call for unripe tomatoes or dig up the whole cordon or bush and hang it upside down in a greenhouse or frost-free shed so that the last ones ripen. Alternatively, cut down the plant from its support, lay it on a bed of straw and cover with a cloche.

Harvesting

Pick the tomatoes as they ripen, which will usually be when they turn red. At this stage they should come away, bringing a short piece of stem, simply by twisting them.

Storage

Tomatoes are best eaten straight from the plants, although they will keep for a few days. They can be frozen, but then used only in cooked dishes as they lose their firmness.

Pests and diseases

Tomatoes are cursed with a number of pests and diseases. Fortunately, they are generally not troublesome enough to deter those who grow them. Pests include aphids, potato cyst eelworm, whitefly and red spider mite. Diseases include tomato blight, grey mould, potato mosaic virus, greenback, tomato leaf mould and scald. Many problems can be avoided by good ventilation. Cracked fruit is often caused by uneven watering.

Cultivation
Indoors
Sowing time early to mid-spring
Sowing inside in modules or pots
Planting time mid- to late spring
Planting and sowing distance 45cm/18in
Harvesting summer onwards
Outdoors
Sowing time inside mid-spring
Planting-out time early summer
Planting distance (cordon) 45cm/18in
Planting distance (bush) 60cm/24in
Distance between sown rows 75cm/30in
Harvesting late summer onwards

Varieties			
Inside	**Inside or outside (cordon)**	'Golden Sunrise'	**Outside (cordon)**
'Aromata'	'Ailsa Craig'	'Harbinger'	'Marmande'
'Big Boy'	'Alicante'	'Mirabelle'	'Outdoor Girl'
'Buffalo'	'Gardener's Delight'	'Moneymaker'	**Outside (bush)**
'Dombito'		'Sungold'	'Golden Sunrise'
'Eurocross'		'Tigarella'	'Ida Gold'
'Grenadier'			'Incas'
'Libra'			'Marmande Super'
'Nimbus'			'Red Alert'
'Shirley'			'The Amateur'
'Super Sweet'			'Tornado'
			'Totem'
			'Tumbler'

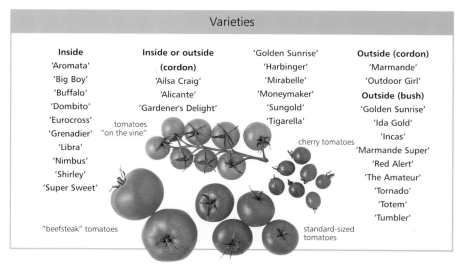

tomatoes "on the vine"

cherry tomatoes

"beefsteak" tomatoes

standard-sized tomatoes

fruit

Fruit can be one of the most enjoyable crops that comes from the kitchen garden, and yet it is probably the most neglected area of gardening. It is difficult to know why this should be the case. In the past, it may have been that fruit was considered to take up too much space, but the modern cultivars now available even make it possible to grow apple trees in containers on a balcony.

One possible reason for people's reluctance to grow fruit is that it can take time to see results. An apple tree may take several years before it produces fruit in any quantity. However, the wait is usually worth it because fresh fruit straight from the plant is one of the great joys of life. Another reason could be that many gardeners are put off by what they see as the complicated art of pruning. But most people perform tasks that are far more complicated than this, and soon pruning becomes second nature.

One point to bear in mind if you are considering planting fruit trees or bushes is that they can be very decorative, especially trained as fans or espaliers, for example. Full-sized fruit trees also have their advantages – they are wonderful for sitting under on hot summer days.

Strawberries
Fragaria × ananassa

Strawberries are one of the best loved fruits. No matter how readily they are available in the supermarkets, there is nothing quite like wandering into the garden and picking a few to eat there and then. The taste is always better, especially if the fruit is still warm from the sun.

It is now possible to pick strawberries from early summer right through to the first frosts and even beyond, if protection is provided. Strawberries are categorized by their time of fruiting and are known as "early", "mid-season" and "late", which continue to fruit well into autumn. There are also perpetual strawberries, which produce fruit in summer, have a break and then start again in autumn. If you have space it is a good idea to plan your strawberry bed so that you have as long a productive season as possible. There are also alpine strawberries, which produce very small fruits over a long period. All strawberry plants should come from certified stock to ensure against virus diseases.

Strawberries are not very difficult to grow. If grown in beds they take up quite a bit of space, but they can also be grown in pots or in towers – a series of containers one on top of the other. They can be grown in a greenhouse, which produces earlier and later crops, but the flavour is not as good as that of crops grown outdoors.

The plants will remain productive for only about three years, and it is important to have a rolling programme to renew a third of the plants each year. Unfortunately, they really need to be planted in fresh ground, so it is not simply a question of taking out one row and replacing it with another; the new plants should ideally go elsewhere in the garden. Alternatively you can create a completely new bed in the third year, and abandon the old one immediately after the fruit has been produced.

Cultivation
Strawberries need an open, sunny site. The soil should be fertile and well drained. The plants should be set out in late summer or early autumn, at intervals of 38cm/15in, with each row 75cm/30in apart. As the plants come into fruit the following year, place clean straw under the leaves and fruiting stems to keep the fruit off the ground. Polythene (plastic) or felt mats will serve the same purpose. Deep water during dry periods.

Pruning and training
Strawberries are not pruned or trained as such, but after fruiting it is normal practice to cut off all the old leaves and burn or destroy these, together with the straw mulch, to remove any pests and diseases. Remove any runners as they are formed unless you want keep a few new plants.

Harvesting
Pick the fruit as it ripens. Pick with a short piece of stalk attached.

Storage
The fruit is best eaten straight from the plants, although it can also be frozen or

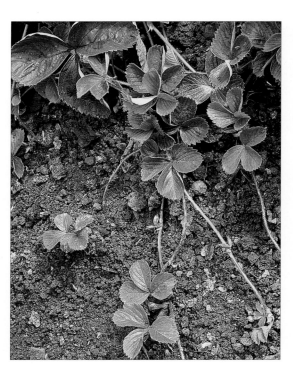

ABOVE **After fruiting, the strawberry plant sends out a series of runners that root along their length to produce new plants.**

bottled. Unfortunately, frozen strawberries go mushy when they defrost.

Pests and diseases
Birds and slugs are two of the worst problems. Birds can be kept at bay if the plants are netted while they are in fruit. Viruses and grey mould can also be problems. Burn or destroy any plant with viral disease.

CARE AFTER FRUITING

After the strawberries have produced their fruit, cut off all the leaves and burn or destroy them, along with the straw mulch. This helps prevent the spread of diseases.

RUNNERS

The strawberry runners have produced a perfect new plant through layering. The layered plants can be dug up once they have rooted and used to start a new bed.

ABOVE **On this plant a succession of stages can be seen, from flowers to ripe fruit. Fruit picked straight from the plant tastes best.**

PROTECTING THE FRUIT

Place a layer of straw under the leaves of the strawberry plants in order to prevent the developing fruit from getting muddy or covered with dirt.

Varieties

Early
'Cambridge Early Pine'
'Cambridge Prizewinner'
'Cambridge Vigour'
'Honeoye'
'Maxim'
Mid-season
'Cambridge Favourite'
'Cambridge Sentry'
'Grandee'
'Hapil'
'Jamil'
'Redgauntlet'
'Tamella'
'Tenira'
Late
'Cambridge Late Pine'
'Domanil'
'Fenland Wonder'

'Merton Dawn'
'Montrose'
'Saladin'
'Le Sans Rivale'
'Symphony'
'Troubadour'

Perpetual (remontant)
'Calypso'
'Mara des Bois'
'Rabunda'
'Red Rich'
'St Claude'
Alpine
'Alexandria'
'Baron Solemacher'
'Delicious'
'Yellow Wonder'

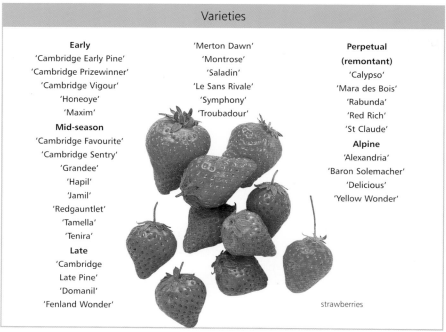

strawberries

Raspberries
Rubus idaeus

Raspberries are an appealing fruit, although they are often overshadowed by strawberries, which come into season at the same time. They are a good fruit for eating straight from the plant or for freezing and for making into jams and preserves. Raspberries can be used in a wide range of cakes and desserts as well as sauces for both sweet and savoury dishes.

It is possible to provide a good "taste" of raspberries by growing a group of just a few canes, but it is more usual to grow the canes in a row. This may take up quite a large amount of space, but it can be used as a hedge or screen, so fulfilling a double function. The canes are tied into wires that are supported on posts, which adds to the initial cost, but once the framework has been erected it will last for a long time, as will the raspberries.

As with strawberries, new varieties of raspberry have been developed so that it is possible to have a supply of fruit from early summer right through to the first frosts, which in a mild year can mean early winter. Rather than having three separate rows, which would take up a great deal of space, it is possible to divide a single row into three or even four separate sections for early, mid-season, late and autumn fruit.

ABOVE **Ripening and immature fruit on a raspberry cane. Ripe raspberries can be obtained over a very long period if the varieties are chosen carefully.**

Cultivation
Like most fruit, raspberries like an open situation with plenty of air circulating among them, but, unlike most other fruit, they will tolerate a little partial shade. The soil should be fertile and moisture retentive, but it should not be waterlogged. Permanent supports in the form of posts and wires should be erected. The wires should be 75cm/30in, 1.1m/3ft 6in and 1.5m/5ft from the ground. Allow 1.5m/5ft between rows. Plant the canes at intervals of 38–45cm/15–18in, spreading out their roots, during late autumn or early winter. Remove any suckers that appear out of the row, and use them as new stock if required. Mulch with garden compost or manure every spring

Pruning and training
Each autumn remove all the old fruiting canes by cutting them off at the base. Tie in the new canes to the wires. In late winter cut off the tip of each cane to a bud about 15cm/6in above the top wire. If you grow autumn-fruiting varieties, cut *all* canes to the ground in late winter.

Harvesting
Pick as the fruit becomes ripe, squeezing gently with the fingers so that the fruit slides off its "plug".

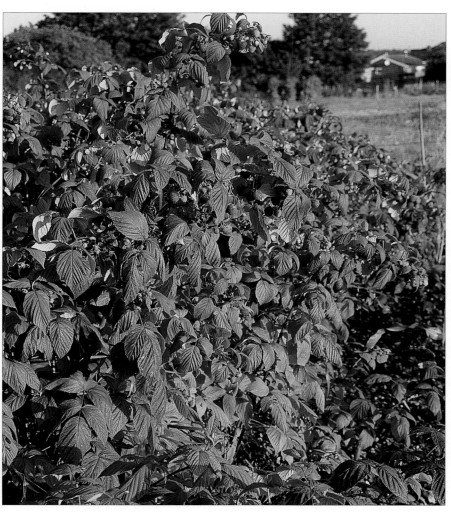

LEFT **If this crop of ripening raspberries is left uncovered in this way, there will be few to eat because the birds will strip them away.**

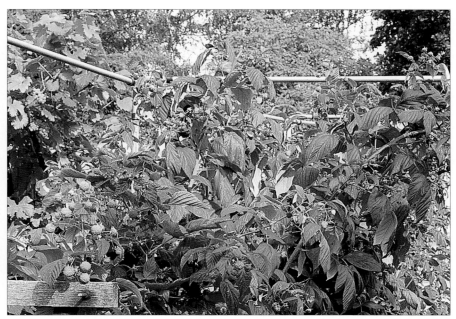

Storage

The fruit is best eaten straight from the plant. However, it can be stored by freezing, bottling or turning into jam or other preserves. Frozen fruit becomes mushy and loses its shape and firmness, although it is still useful as fillings and sauces. You can overcome the storage problem by selecting and growing a range of varieties. This means you will have a continuous supply of fresh fruit from early summer right through to the first frost.

Pests and diseases

Birds are a nuisance unless the raspberry canes are netted or protected in a fruit cage. Raspberry beetle – the grub is found in the fruit – is often a nuisance. Spray with derris as soon as the first fruits begin to ripen, and then make a second application two weeks later. Grey mould can cause the fruit to rot and there is also the possibility of some virus diseases. Infected canes should be removed and either burned or destroyed.

ABOVE **This double row of raspberries is supported by wires that are secured on a well-constructed wooden framework.**

ABOVE LEFT **These raspberry canes are tied into wire supports by twisting a continuous piece of string around the wire in order to trap the canes.**

Varieties	
Early	'Malling Orion'
'Delight'	**Late**
'Glen Clova'	'Augusta'
'Glen Coe'	'Leo'
'Glen Moy'	'Malling
'Malling Exploit'	Admiral'
'Malling Promise'	'Malling Joy'
'Sumner'	**Autumn**
Mid-season	'Autumn Bliss'
'Glen Lyon'	'Fallgold'
'Glen Prosen'	'Heritage'
'Julia'	'Norfolk Giant'
'Malling Jewel'	'September'

raspberries

Growing raspberries on posts and wires It is essential that raspberries have a strong supporting system of posts and wires. The plants are set at 38–45cm/15–18in intervals. Each year, new raspberry canes are thrown up. When fruiting has finished on the old canes, these are cut out and the new canes are tied to the wires in their place. This sequence is followed every year. Raspberry plants put out suckers which can become established in the gangways between the rows. These should be dug up as soon as they appear.

Blackberries and Hybrid Berries
Rubus fruticosus

Although blackberries that are picked in the wild have a great deal to offer, there are advantages to be gained from growing cultivated forms. The first is that they are conveniently at hand. Second, the fruit is usually much larger and often sweeter. Then there is the fact that you can get thornless varieties, which makes picking much easier. A disadvantage, however, is that you do need quite a bit of space to grow them successfully, although they do not need to be a free-standing crop. They can, for example, be grown along a boundary fence, which may well be a good use of space as well as acting as a deterrent to intruders.

ABOVE **Blackberries fruit over a long season, as is shown by a sprig of ripe and immature blackberries.**

RIGHT **This vigorous stand of blackberries shows the prodigious nature of many of these plants.**

Cultivated blackberries are derived from their wild relatives; the hybrid berries are crosses between various *Rubus* species, often involving blackberries and raspberries in their parentage. Each of these berries, including loganberries, boysenberries and tayberries, has a distinctive flavour and is grown in the same manner as blackberries.

They come into fruit from late summer onwards and are, therefore, available later than most other soft fruit, which is another advantage. Like most fruit, blackberries and hybrid berries are best eaten straight from the garden, but they can also be used in a wide range of dessert dishes and sauces.

Blackberries are usually grown on post and wire supports, the wires being placed at 38cm/15in intervals up to about 1.8m/6ft. The thornless varieties are not as vigorous and take up less space. In a really large garden, blackberries could be left to grow free, like their wild cousins, but this is not recommended because cultivated varieties are often much more vigorous than wild forms.

Cultivation

Blackberries prefer a sunny spot, but will grow in a modicum of partial shade. The soil should be well prepared, with plenty of added humus. Plant the canes in late winter or early spring, placing them 3.5–4.5m/ 12–15ft apart (thornless varieties can be closer together), and immediately shorten them to a bud about 23–30cm/9–12in above ground. Do not plant deeply; the soil should only just cover the roots, which should be spread out in the planting hole. Mulch with manure in the spring and water in dry weather. They can be increased by bending down a vigorous shoot and planting its tip to form a layer. A new plant will quickly form and can be severed from the parent.

Pruning and training

In autumn cut out all the old fruiting stems and tie in the new growth. There are several methods of training blackberries and hybrid berries. One is to tie in all of one year's growth to one side, several canes to each wire, and the new growth to the other side. Another is to tie the fruiting growth along the wires, allowing the new growth to grow up the middle. A more formal and higher yielding method is to create a fan, with the shoots tied in a radiating pattern from the base, again leaving the centre free for new growth.

Harvesting

Pick as fruit becomes ripe, without any stalks.

Storage

Fresh blackberries last a day or so but can be frozen, bottled or used in preserves.

Pests and diseases

Blackberries are prone to the same problems as raspberries.

Alternate bay One way to train blackberries is to tie all the new growth to one side of the wirework. After fruiting, remove the previous year's growth from the other side and then use this for the next year's new growth. Repeat each year.

Rope training A second way to train blackberries is to temporarily tie in all new growth vertically to the wirework and along the top wire. The current fruiting canes are tied in groups horizontally. These are removed after fruiting and the new growth tied into their place.

Fan training The new canes are temporarily tied vertically and along the top wire, while the fruiting canes are tied in singly along the wires. Any excess canes are removed. After fruiting, these canes are taken out and the new growth tied into their place.

Varieties

Blackberries	'Merton Thornless'	Marionberry
'Ashton Cross'	'Oregon Thornless'	Sunberry
'Bedford Giant' – early	'Smoothstem'	Tayberry
'Himalayan Giant'	'Thornfree'	Tummelberry
'John Innes'	**Hybrid berries**	Vietchberry
'Loch Ness'	Boysenberry	Worcesterberry
'Merton Early'	Loganberry	

tayberries

blackberries

Red and White Currants

Ribes rubrum

The only difference between red and white currants is the colour of the fruit. Both types of currant have a very distinctive, slightly tart flavour, but, unlike many other types of fruit, they have a comparatively short season, around midsummer. Red currants in particular are very attractive, and the bushes can be trained into standards, cordons or fans and used as a decorative feature.

As well as being used as fruit in their own right, both are widely used as decoration on cakes and in a wide range of desserts and savoury dishes.

Cultivation

Both red and white currants prefer a sunny site and a rich, moisture-retentive soil. Plant between autumn and early spring at intervals of 1.2–1.5m/4–5ft. Cordons can be 30cm/12in apart and fans can be 1.8m/ 6ft apart. Mulch in spring with well-rotted organic material. Propagate from hardwood cuttings taken in early autumn.

Pruning and training

Initially, prune back all main stems to four buds. After that, prune in spring and summer, reducing the growth on the new leader by about half and that on laterals to about 8cm/3in in spring and to four or five leaves in summer. Once the bushes are established, cut back all side shoots to one bud and take the tip out of the main stems. Let new shoots from the base replace older wood. If you are growing them as cordons, in early spring remove a third of the new growth on the leader and cut back laterals to three buds. In summer cut back all laterals to five leaves.

Harvesting and storage

Pick when the currants are ripe, taking the whole cluster of fruit. They can be frozen or turned into preserves – but remove the stalks first.

Pests and diseases

Birds, which will attack both buds and fruit, are likely to be the biggest problem. Aphids and black currant gall mites may also be troublesome. Grey mould may be a problem and coral spot can affect the branches.

BELOW **These cordons of red and white currants have been tied to vertical canes which are, in turn, tied to horizontal wires.**

Pruning a red or white currant cordon On planting, cut back the leader by half of its new growth and cut back the side shoots to one bud. Thereafter, cut back the side shoots every summer to five leaves and, in winter, further reduce these to one bud.

Pruning a red or white currant bush After planting, cut back each shoot by about half. Subsequent pruning involves ensuring that the plant becomes an open bush. Cut back all new growth on the main shoots and reduce the new growth on all side shoots to one bud.

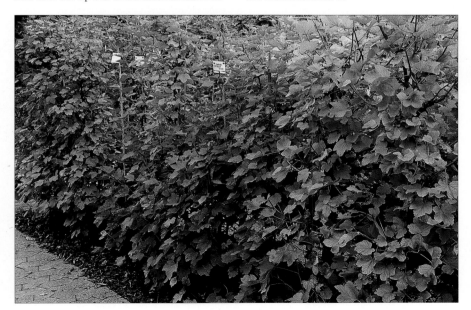

Varieties	
Red currants	**White currants**
'Jonkheer van Tets'	'Versailles Blanche'
'Junifer'	'White Dutch'
'Laxton's Number 1'	'White Grape'
'Red Lake'	'White Pearl'
'Redstart'	
'Rondom'	
'Rovada'	

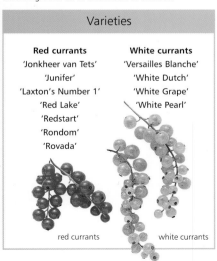

red currants   white currants

Blackcurrants
Ribes nigrum

Not only do blackcurrants have a unique flavour, but they are much valued for their high vitamin C content. They are used widely in desserts as well as jams and drinks. Blackcurrants, like red and white currants, tend to have a relatively short season compared with other soft fruit, but although related to red currants it is important to realize that they are pruned in a different way. Because the fruit is produced on the previous season's growth, it is important that this is not removed. Unlike red currants, blackcurrants can only be grown on bushes.

They are long-lived plants, lasting up to 15 years or more. Joostberries, a cross between blackcurrants and gooseberries, are grown in the same way.

Cultivation

Blackcurrants prefer a sunny site, although they will tolerate a little light shade. The soil should be well prepared and have plenty of well-rotted humus added to it. Plant between autumn and early spring, setting the plants at intervals of 1.5m/5ft. Mulch in spring with a layer of organic material. Water during dry spells but not when the fruit starts to ripen or it may split. Propagate from hardwood cuttings taken in autumn.

Pruning and training

After planting, reduce all shoots to one bud above the ground. The following winter remove any weak wood. After that remove any weak wood and up to a third of the older wood so that new growth is produced. Never reduce the lengths of the shoots.

Harvesting and storage

Pick the fruit as it ripens, retaining the stalks. Store by freezing or preserving, removing all stalks first.

Pests and diseases

Birds are likely to be the biggest problem. Aphids, big bud mite and gall mites may also be troublesome. Leaf spot and powdery mildew can also be a problem.

RIGHT **Blackcurrants and red currants are usually picked in bunches, complete with their stalks. They can be collected in a trug for convenience.**

Varieties	
'Baldwin'	'Malling Jet'
'Ben Connan'	'Mendip Cross'
'Ben Lomond'	'Wellington XXX'
'Ben More'	
'Ben Sarek'	
'Boskoop Giant'	

blackcurrants

Pruning a blackcurrant bush After planting, cut blackcurrant bushes back to a single bud above the ground. The following winter, remove any weak or misplaced growth. Subsequent pruning should take place after fruiting and consists of cutting out up to a third of two-year-old or older wood in order to stimulate new growth. Also remove any weak or misplaced stems.

Gooseberries
Ribes uva-crispa

Because most people think that gooseberries need cooking and so do not fit into the world of convenience foods, they are not, perhaps, as popular as they were in the past. This is a pity, partly because gooseberries have a very distinctive flavour, suitable for a range of dishes and sauces, but also because gooseberries can be eaten raw – there are some delicious dessert varieties. Unfortunately, these rarely find their way into shops, and so it is only gardeners who are likely to appreciate them – an excellent reason for growing your own.

Gooseberries are easy plants to grow, the only drawback being the thorns, which can be very sharp, but well-trained bushes and the use of cordons make it easier to get at the fruit without being torn to pieces. Typical gooseberries are green, but there are also red and yellow varieties.

Cultivation
Gooseberries require an open, sunny position, although they will take some light shade. The soil should contain plenty of well-rotted organic material. Plant the bushes at any time between autumn and early spring when the weather and soil are favourable. They should be set 1.5m/5ft apart. Mulch in spring with a good layer of manure. Avoid hoeing because the roots are only just below the surface and can be damaged. New plants can be propagated by hardwood cuttings taken in autumn.

Pruning and training
Gooseberries can be grown as bushes, cordons or standards. They are treated in the same way as red currants. Keep the centre of the bush open so that plenty of air can circulate as well as making it easier to get at the fruit.

Harvesting and storage
Start harvesting before the fruit is quite ripe. Such fruit can be cooked or frozen. Wait until fruit is fully ripe if it is for eating raw. Continue picking as the fruit ripens. Pick with a stalk, although this must be removed before storing. Store by freezing, bottling or by making jam or other preserves.

Pruning a gooseberry The basic aim when pruning gooseberries is to create an open framework. Establish a framework, first of all, by removing the basal shoots and cutting back the main shoots by about half in their first and second years. After this, cut back the new growth on the leaders in winter by about half and reduce the side shoots from these to two buds. Remove any damaged wood and any branches that cross or rub. Remove suckers and basal growth. In summer, prune the side shoots back to five leaves, but leave the main stems uncut.

Pests and diseases
One the whole, gooseberries are not prone to a great many pests and diseases. The main problem is powdery mildew, and one way to prevent this is to ensure that plenty of air can circulate around and through the bushes. Birds can also be a nuisance in spring when they strip off buds.

Varieties

'Broom Girl'	'Lancashire Lad'
'Careless'	'Leveller'
'Early Sulphur'	'Whinham's Industry'
'Greenfinch'	'White Lion'
'Invicta'	'Whitesmith'
'Jubilee'	'Yellow Champagne'

gooseberries

LEFT **Gooseberries can be grown as single cordons. This is achieved by tying them into canes which are supported by horizontal wires.**

Blueberries
Vaccinium corymbosum

The high-bush blueberry is becoming more popular in the garden. The rich, fruity flavour that is a characteristic of the berries has made it popular as a fruit to be eaten straight from the bush and for inclusion in an ever-increasing number of desserts and other dishes. Its disadvantage as a garden fruit, at least for some people, is that it must have acid conditions. In chalky or limestone (alkaline) regions bushes could be grown in large containers away from the normal garden soil, but this could become quite a chore, no matter how tasty the resulting berries.

The bushes and berries are decorative and are a useful addition in the potager or ornamental border.

Cultivation
Choose a sunny site, although a little light, partial shade will be tolerated. The soil must be acidic. Add ericaceous compost (soil mix) if your garden soil is just on the borderline. Set out the plants at any time the weather and soil conditions allow between autumn and early spring. Plant them as free-standing bushes, 1.5m/5ft apart. Mulch with manure, but only if it has not been "sweetened" with chalk or limestone. An ericaceous compost can be used or marginally acid soil. Do not allow the soil to become dry, watering regularly as necessary. Propagate from softwood cuttings taken in midsummer.

Pruning and training
Because the fruit appears on the second- or third-year wood, do not prune until cropping starts. After that, cut out any dead or weak wood and then remove up to a third of the oldest wood to promote new growth. Prune in winter or early spring.

Harvesting and storage
Pick as the fruit ripens and store, if necessary, by freezing or bottling.

Pests and diseases
Blueberries are remarkably trouble free. The worst problem will be birds, which will steal the fruit, but netting will solve this.

ABOVE **This healthy looking cluster of ripening blueberries clearly shows the distinctive powdery bloom of the fruit which most gardeners try to retain when picking.**

BELOW **A vigorous blueberry bush, such as this, with plenty of ripening fruit, must be protected to stop birds from stripping away the fruit before it ripens.**

Pruning an established blueberry bush Blueberries fruit on older wood, so no pruning is needed for several years. Thereafter, cut out any weak or misplaced shoots as well as the old wood that has ceased fruiting in order to stimulate new growth.

Varieties

'Berkeley'	'Goldtraube'
'Bluecrop'	'Herbert'
'Bluejay'	'Patriot'
'Bluetta'	'Spartan'
'Duke'	

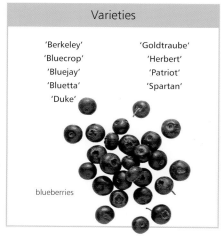

blueberries

Apples
Malus domestica

Apples are a staple fruit, grown in many countries around the world, but although there are, literally, thousands of varieties, the number available in shops can be limited. Unlike many other fruits, in which the taste is only marginally different from one variety to another, apples exhibit a great range of flavours and textures. Some are suitable for cooking, others are dessert (eating) apples, and others combine these qualities.

To help you choose among the vast range of apple varieties, visit one of the open days held by specialist apple nurseries and collectors. It is usually possible to taste several different varieties of ripe fruit and see the trees themselves, which you can often buy or order.

One aspect of apple growing that may restrict your choice is pollination. Most apples need another variety to pollinate them, and because the flowering time varies from variety to variety it is essential to choose two that flower during the same period.

Another question that will have to be addressed is what type of plant do you want. The old standard trees look best and produce a heavy crop, but they are usually too large for today's smaller garden, and ladders are needed for pruning and harvesting. Cordons take up the least space, but the crop is small. On the other hand, cordons allow you to have several different varieties in a small space. There are, however, all kinds of shapes and sizes between the two extremes, some of them very decorative. Always check the rootstock of the plants you buy to see how vigorous and large the tree will be ultimately.

Cultivation

Apple trees will be in position for years, so prepare the soil well, adding plenty of organic material. An open, sunny position is best. Plant young trees at any time of year between late autumn and early spring, as long as weather and soil conditions are favourable. The planting distances vary considerably depending on the type and size of tree. Cordons, for example, may be only 75cm/30in apart, whereas the full standards can be 10m/30ft or more apart, so check first with your supplier. Stake young trees, especially in a windy position. Newly planted trees should not be allowed to dry out. Mulch around the tree every spring with organic material. If necessary protect the blossom from late frosts with fleece.

BELOW **These pole apples have been grown as vertical cordons. The bottoms of the trunks have been protected against attacks by rabbits.**

Rootstocks

The rootstock on an apple tree affects the size and rate of growth of the tree.

M27 an extreme dwarfing stock (bush, dwarf pyramid, cordon)

M9 dwarfing stock (bush, dwarf pyramid, cordon)

M26 semi-dwarfing stock (bush, dwarf pyramid, cordon)

MM106 semi-dwarfing stock (bush, spindle bush, cordon, fan espalier)

M7 semi-dwarfing stock (bush, spindle bush, cordon, fan espalier)

M4 semi-vigorous stock (bush, spindle bush)

MM4 vigorous stock (standard)

M2 vigorous stock

MM111 vigorous stock (half-standard, standard, large bush, large fans, large espaliers)

M25 vigorous stock (standard)

MM109 vigorous stock

M1 vigorous stock

Thin the apples in early and midsummer if there are too many of them – a good guide is to ensure that individual fruits should not touch each other. If branches begin to sag under the weight of fruit, the fruit may need thinning or the branches may need to be supported.

Spur pruning an apple bush tree After planting, cut back the leader to about 75cm/30in above the ground. Leave any side shoots that appear just below this cut and remove any others lower down. The following year, reduce all new growth by about half. This will form the basic framework. Subsequent pruning is restricted to reducing the length of new growth by about a third and removing overcrowded growth.

Pruning and training

Pruning is not difficult once you have done it the first time. Apple trees fall into two groups, depending on where the fruit is borne. On tip bearers the fruit develops near the tip of the shoots, so it is, obviously, important that you cut back shoots in spring. Trees in the other group produce fruit on spurs, which are found on older wood. Most training and pruning involves cutting out dead or weak wood and maintaining the shape and open nature of the tree. Larger trees are pruned in winter only, but those with a more controlled shape need to be pruned in both winter and summer.

Harvesting and storing

Apples should be picked when ripe, which is usually when the fruit comes away easily with a quick twist of the wrist. Some apples store better than others; in general, early apples do not store as well as later ones. If possible, store in a dark, dry, cool place, and ensure the fruits do not touch. Only store sound fruit. Freezing is appropriate for apples that have already been cooked and puréed.

Pests and diseases

A wide range of pests and diseases can affect the trees and fruit. Birds, wasps and codling moths are three of the most important pests. Canker is one of the worst diseases.

Varieties	
Dessert (eating)	'Millers Seedling'
'Blenheim Orange'	'Ribston Pippin'
'Cox's Orange Pippin'	'Starking'
'Discovery'	'Sturmer Pippin'
'Egremont Russet'	'Worcester Pearmain'
'George Cave'	**Cooking**
'Idared'	'Bramley's Seedling'
'James Grieve'	'Grenadier'
'Jonathan'	'Howgate Wonder'
'Laxton's Fortune'	'Lord Darby'
'Laxton's Superb'	'Newton Wonder'
'Lord Lambourne'	

apples

Planting and pruning an apple cordon Cordons are planted as feather maidens at 45° to the wirework. All side shoots are cut back to three buds on planting. Subsequent summer pruning (above right) consists of cutting back any new side shoots to three leaves and new growth on existing side shoots to one leaf. Winter pruning consists of thinning out any of the older spurs if they have become congested.

Pears
Pyrus communis

In the past, pears were, like apples, widely grown, partly for eating and cooking, and partly for turning into perry, a drink akin to cider. Pears for cooking and perry did not have to be the luscious juicy ones that are wanted for eating, and so many people have inherited trees in their gardens that bear pears that are as hard as bullets. This, unfortunately, has put them off growing pears altogether, which is a shame, because ripe eating pears, picked straight from tree can be mouth-watering.

Pears can be grown as standard or dwarf trees as well as in the form of cordons, espaliers and fans. For the smaller garden, cordons are ideal as they make it possible to have several different varieties in a relatively small area. This means that you do not have a glut of one variety but can spread the harvest over a longer period. Pears need warmth to grow well, which is one reason that they are frequently grown against a wall. The warmth is needed not only during the spring at blossom time – they flower early and are particularly susceptible to frosts – but also during summer and autumn so that the fruit can ripen properly. In cold years, when the pears remain hard, they can still be cooked, often by poaching, to make them soft and edible.

Pear trees are vigorous and are, therefore, often unsuitable for small gardens and for some of the smaller forms in which the trees are grown. It is more usual to grow a

ABOVE **Conference pears have a distinctive elongated shape. These healthy specimens are ripe for picking and enjoying.**

pear tree that has been grafted onto a quince rootstock to curb its vigour. This means that any suckers appearing below the graft should be removed.

As with apples, pears must be grown near a different variety so that the blossom can be pollinated. Unless there happens to be a compatible tree in a neighbouring garden, you will have to plant at least two trees. Unfortunately, you cannot use any variety – the trees must be compatible. Consult your supplier about suitable pairs.

Cultivation
Pear trees must have a sheltered, warm site and fertile, free-draining, but moisture-retentive, soil. Add plenty of organic material while preparing the ground. Set out new plants at any time between late autumn and spring with favourable weather and soil conditions. Planting distances vary according to the type of plant. Bush trees can be up to 4.5m/15ft apart, dwarf pyramids 1.5m/5ft apart, cordons 75cm/30in apart, and espaliers and fans 4.5m/15ft apart. Stake free-standing trees to prevent wind-rock. Mulch with manure in the spring. Thoroughly water during dry spells. If the crop is heavy, thin out young fruit in early to midsummer so that they do not touch.

Pruning and training
Most varieties of pears are spur-bearers, which means that they produce fruit on spurs that grow on two-year-old or older wood. The leader's new growth can, therefore, be safely cut back in winter by about a third of its length, and laterals can be pruned to three or four buds. Spurs are readily produced and

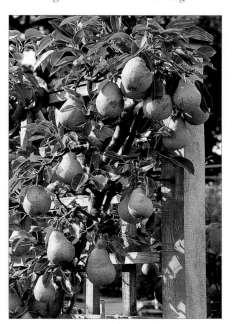

LEFT **These pears have been grown in a cordon against trellis, a method suitable for small gardens.**

should be thinned once the tree is established. Before starting to prune and shape a tree, always remove any dead, dying or weak growth and then work with what is left.

Harvesting and storage
The picking time for pears is crucial. The fruit should be just ripe; any that is left on the tree beyond this stage will soon become overripe. Pick as soon as the fruit comes away readily to a twisting motion of the hand. Early varieties can be picked just before they ripen, but mid-season and late varieties should be left until they are ripe. Pears can be stored in slatted trays in a cool room. Only store sound fruit and position them so that they do not touch each other.

Rootstocks

As with apples, the rootstock on which a pear tree grows affects the size and rate of growth of the tree.
Quince C moderately dwarfing stock (bush, cordon, dwarf pyramid, espalier, fan)
Quince A semi-vigorous stock (bush, cordon, dwarf pyramid, espalier, fan)
Pear vigorous stock (standards, half-standards)

RIGHT **A pear tree trained in the shape of a cone.**

Pruning an espaliered pear After planting, cut back to two buds above the bottom wire. In the first summer, tie the central growth to a vertical cane and the next two shoots to canes at 45°. Cut back all other shoots to two leaves. In autumn, lower the two side shoots to the horizontal and tie the cane to the bottom wire. In winter, cut back the leader to two buds above the second wire and repeat the above until the espalier covers all the wires. When established, cut back all new shoots to three leaves each summer.

Pruning a dwarf pyramid pear After planting, cut back the leader by about a third. Cut side shoots back to about 15cm/6in. In the first summer, cut back the new growth on the main side shoots to about five leaves and on the secondary shoots to three leaves. Thereafter, cut back new growth on the main stems to five leaves and reduce other new growth to one leaf. During the winter, thin out any congested spurs.

Pests and diseases

Pears are prone to a number of problems, including aphids, codling moth and pear midge. Diseases include fireblight, canker, scab and brown rot. Fireblight will probably mean the removal of the entire tree; it must then be burned or destroyed. For other pests and diseases, check on the latest controls with your local nursery or garden centre.

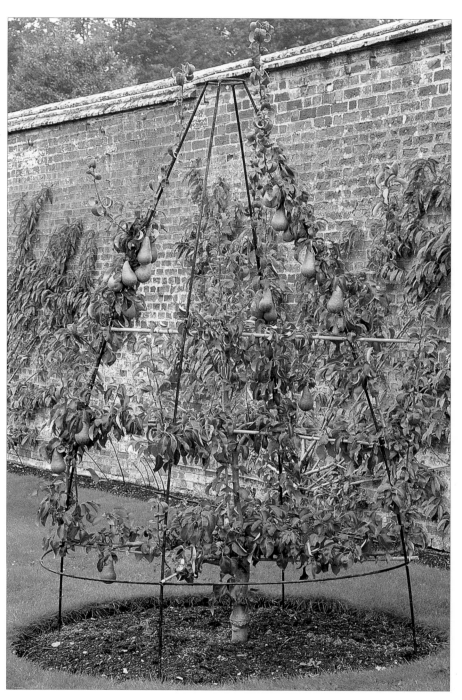

Varieties

'Beth'	'Glou Morceau'
'Beurré Hardy'	'Jargonelle'
'Black Worcester'	'Joséphine de Malines'
'Concorde'	'Louise Bonne of Jersey'
'Conference'	'Merton Pride'
'Doyenné du Comice'	'Onward'
'Durondeau'	'Williams' Bon Chrétien'

pears

Plums
Prunus domestica

Plums are one of the great unexplored parts of the fruit world. In the past there were many different varieties, all with different flavours and textures, but now all knowledge of such fruit seems to have been lost. At most, one or two varieties surface occasionally in shops, but few people seem to know of the treasury of delights that could be available. Fortunately, many of the old varieties are available from specialist nurseries, and anyone who takes the trouble to search them out is really in for a treat.

The name "plum" actually encompasses a great diversity of fruit, including damsons, bullaces and the gages. Plums come in all shapes and sizes as well as a range of colours, from red to black and from yellow to green. The flesh, too, varies from red to yellow. As with the other main tree fruits, distinctive cultivars have been developed for dessert (eating uncooked) purposes and for cooking. The former are succulent and mouthwatering; the latter are firmer and less sweet.

In general, plums like a sunny situation, but there are plums for all sorts of climates and you may well find that some are better suited to local conditions than others.

ABOVE **A cluster of plums that would have benefited from thinning out – they are growing too close together and could have filled out more.**

Check to see what varieties are still grown in your neighbourhood area and what may have been grown in the past when they were more widely grown.

Plums are mainly grown as trees, varying from full-sized standards to spindle bushes and pyramids. They can also be trained as fans. Unfortunately, they cannot be grown as cordons. Plums trees are not usually large and can be accommodated, even in small gardens.

Damsons were traditionally grown as hedgerow trees and can be planted in a hedge, saving a lot of space and yet producing a good crop of fruit. Plums vary in fertility, some being self-fertile, but they all do better for having a pollinator in the area.

Cultivation

Plums must have a sunny position; in cooler areas, a position against a wall will be ideal. They flower early and so should not be planted in frost pockets, where the blossom will be lost. The soil should be

Pruning a plum fan in spring and summer The main aim when pruning a plum fan is to maintain the fan shape. In spring, cut out any new side shoots that are pointing to or away from the wall. If necessary, reduce the number of new shoots to about one every 15cm/6in. In summer, cut back all new shoots to about six leaves, leaving any that are needed to fill in gaps in the main framework. In autumn, after cropping, further cut back the shoots to three leaves.

Rootstocks

The rootstock on which a plum tree grows affects the size and rate of growth.

Pixy dwarfing stock (bush, pyramid)
Damas C moderately vigorous stock
St Julien A semi-vigorous stock
(bush, fan, pyramid)
Brompton A vigorous stock
(half-standards, standards)
Myrobalan B vigorous stock
(half-standards, standards)

Varieties	
Dessert	'Merton Gem'
'Ariel'	'Oullin's Gage'
'Cambridge Gage'	'Victoria'
'Coe's Golden Drop'	**Cooking**
'Early Laxton'	'Belle de Louvain'
'Greengage'	'Czar'
'Jefferson'	'Early Rivers'
'Kirke's Blue'	'Laxton's Cropper'
'Marjorie's Seedling'	'Pershore Yellow'

red plums

yellow plums

fertile and moisture retentive, although they will tolerate drier soil than many other tree fruits. Plant the trees at any time between autumn and early spring, as long as weather and soil conditions allow. Planting distance will vary from 3m/10ft to 7.5m/25ft, depending on the size of tree. Fan-trained trees will need to be 3–4.5m/10–15ft apart. Smaller trees and fan-trained varieties should be covered if frost threatens while they are in blossom. Mulch in early spring with a good layer of organic material. If the crop is heavy, thin the fruit as soon as the stones begin to form. Thin so that they are 5–8cm/2–3in apart.

Pruning and training

Any pruning should be carried out in summer to reduce the chances of the tree being infected with silver leaf. Once the initial shape has been determined, larger trees do not need any pruning apart from the removal of dead or damaged wood. On fans, remove all new shoots that face towards or away from the wall. Shorten any retained new growth to six leaves.

Harvesting and storage

Pick the plums as they ripen. For cooking and preserving pick a little earlier, just before the fruit is ripe. Keep the stalk on the fruit as you pick them. They can be frozen or bottled for storage, but it is best to remove the stones first.

Pests and diseases

Wasps and birds can cause problems as can larger animals such as rabbits and hares. Other insect pests include aphids and winter moths. The main diseases are silver leaf, canker and brown rot. Trees that are affected with silver leaf and canker should be burnt or destroyed at once.

ABOVE **Ripening damsons are suitable for cooking once they have coloured. Eat fresh when fully ripe.**

Peaches and Nectarines

Prunus persica and P. p. var. nectarina

Peaches and nectarines are closely related, the main difference between the two is that peaches have a downy skin, while nectarines are smooth skinned. They are treated similarly in the garden, although nectarines do better in warmer conditions and are less hardy.

Both fruits can be grown as free-standing trees, but in cooler climates both are better grown as fans against a warm, south-facing wall or even a solid fence.

Cultivation

Peaches and nectarines need a warm, sunny site. The soil should be free draining, but it is also important that it is moisture retentive, so plenty of organic material should be added to the soil. Plant the trees or fans in autumn or early winter, with both at a distance of 4.5m/15ft. Trees should be staked to avoid wind-rock. Mulch in the spring with a good layer of manure or garden compost. If frosts are forecast when they are in blossom, cover the plants with fleece or polythene (plastic) frames. Water during dry periods.

It may be necessary to assist pollination by hand pollinating. Use a soft brush to transfer pollen from the anthers of one flower to the stigmas of another. The flowers should be fully open and the weather dry and warm. With a good fruit set it will be necessary to thin them, removing the excess fruits so that they are 15cm/6in apart.

Pruning and training

Mature trees do not require much pruning apart from the removal of dead or damaged wood and the cutting out of some of the older wood to promote new, vigorous growth. Remove all the shoots that face towards or away from the wall. Initially, thin other shoots to intervals of about 15cm/6in, tying them to the wires and removing the tips if they are longer than about 45cm/18in. Once the plant is established, allow a new bud to form at the base of each lateral in spring, but remove all other buds.

After fruiting, remove the fruiting wood and tie in the new lateral to replace it. Remove the tip if it is too long.

Harvesting and storing

Pick the fruit as it ripens. They are best eaten straight from the tree but can be kept for a few days in a cool place. They can be stored for longer periods by freezing or bottling.

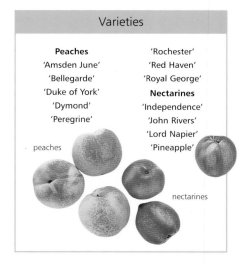

Varieties

Peaches	'Rochester'
'Amsden June'	'Red Haven'
'Bellegarde'	'Royal George'
'Duke of York'	**Nectarines**
'Dymond'	'Independence'
'Peregrine'	'John Rivers'
	'Lord Napier'
peaches	'Pineapple'

peaches

nectarines

Pests and diseases

Birds and aphids can be a common problem with peaches and nectarines as can earwigs and red spider mites. Diseases include peach leaf curl, powdery mildew and canker.

Peach bush tree Not a great deal of pruning is required for a peach bush tree. In spring, cut back some of the older barren wood as far as a replacement new shoot. Also remove any awkwardly placed branches and keep the bush open and airy. Avoid making large cuts, as this is likely to allow canker to infect the tree.

LEFT **Fan-trained peaches such as this healthy specimen provide a decorative feature for a wall.**

Rootstocks

The rootstock will affect the size and rate of growth of the tree.
St Julien A semi-vigorous stock (bush, fan)
Brompton A vigorous stock (bush)

Apricots
Prunus armeniaca

Apricots are not grown as frequently as most other fruit, partly because they are not very easy to grow and partly because, with limited space, most gardeners prefer to grow the more luscious peaches. Home-grown apricots may well be a revelation, however, because they taste much better than shop-bought fruit ever does.

One of the problems with apricots is that they flower very early and are susceptible to frosts. They are, therefore, suitable only for warm areas. Their need for warmth means that they are best grown as fans against a south-facing wall, which will help to protect them from the cold. They are self-fertile, so there is no need for different varieties and only one tree need be grown if space is limited.

Cultivation

A warm, sunny, frost-free site is required to grow apricots successfully. The soil should be free draining but moisture retentive. You will have to incorporate plenty of organic material before planting. Plant in autumn or early winter, placing fans about 4.5m/15ft apart. The blossom will need to be protected if there is the possibility of frost. Mulch the ground with a good layer of

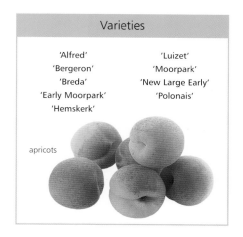

Varieties

'Alfred' 'Luizet'
'Bergeron' 'Moorpark'
'Breda' 'New Large Early'
'Early Moorpark' 'Polonais'
'Hemskerk'

apricots

manure and keep the ground watered during dry spells. If there is a potentially heavy crop, thin out the fruits to about 8cm/3in apart.

Pruning and training

On mature fans pinch out the laterals in summer to about 8cm/3in. Remove any laterals that face towards or away from the wall. Later, in summer, remove any more laterals that have developed. Apart from that, little pruning is required because most apricot fruit is borne on old wood. Every few years, remove some of the older wood and allow new laterals to develop in order to replace it.

Harvesting and storage

Pick the fruit once it has fully ripened and can be removed easily from the stalk. Apricots do not store well, although they can be frozen or dried.

Pests and diseases

Protect fruit from birds by netting. Aphids may also be a problem. The most likely diseases are silver leaf, canker, brown rot and die back.

Apricot fan Once the fan has been established, the object of most subsequent pruning is to maintain the shape. Cut out any shoots that are pointing in the wrong direction, especially those that point towards or away from the wall. Thin new shoots, leaving one every 15cm/6in. Prune the remaining shoots to five leaves in the spring and then again, after fruiting, back to three leaves.

LEFT **An elegant fan-trained apricot spread out across a large wall. The canes, supported by wires, help to maintain the fan shape.**

Rootstocks

The rootstock will affect the size and rate of growth of the tree.
St Julien A semi-vigorous stock (bush, fan)
Brompton A vigorous stock (bush)

GARDENING CALENDAR

Winter

AW *all winter* EW *early winter* MW *midwinter*
LW *late winter*

Spring

AS *all spring* ES *early spring* MS *mid-spring*
LS *late spring*

Summer

AS *all summer* ES *early summer* MS *midsummer*
LS *late summer*

General

Clean and maintain tools and equipment AW
Plan next year's crops AW
Order seed and plants AW
Order sowing and potting composts (soil mixes) AW
Order manure AW
Continue digging soil when conditions allow AW
Avoid treading or working on waterlogged soil AW
Clean and prepare pots and propagators AW
Compost any organic waste AW

General

Prepare seed beds AS
Finish winter digging and ground preparation ES
Keep weeds under control AS
Water in dry weather LS

General

Keep weeds under control AS
Water when necessary AS
Keep an eye out for pests and diseases AS
Take soft and semi-ripe cuttings MS–LS

Vegetables

Sow early vegetables under glass for planting
under protection MW–LW
Sow early vegetables for planting out LW
Check stored vegetables AW
Plant rhubarb MW–LW
Sow broad (fava) beans MW–LW
Sow parsnips if conditions allow LW
Plant early potatoes if conditions allow LW
Protect overwintering crops such as peas and broad
(fava) beans with cloches AW
Protect brassicas from birds AW
Force rhubarb LW

Vegetables

Mulch permanent beds with manure ES–MS
Begin main sowing and planting of hardy vegetables AS
Continue successional sowings MS–LS
Sow tender vegetables like runner beans under glass LS
Plant tomatoes, aubergines (eggplants), cucumbers and
peppers in heated greenhouses ES–MS
Plant tomatoes, aubergines (eggplants), cucumbers and
peppers in unheated greenhouses MS–LS
Plant Jerusalem artichokes, potatoes and onions ES–MS
Plant permanent crops such as globe artichokes
and asparagus ES
Plant out tender vegetables after last frosts LS
Protect vulnerable new growth from frosts AS
Erect supports for peas and beans MS–LS
Force rhubarb ES
Mulch vegetables LS

Vegetables

Plant out greenhouse-sown tender vegetables ES
Sow tender vegetables ES
Sow winter crops MS–LS
Continue successional sowings ES–MS
Harvest early vegetables as required AS
Shade and ventilate greenhouse vegetables AS
Dampen greenhouse floor to maintain humidity AS
Pick greenhouse vegetables as they ripen AS
Pinch out side shoots from tomatoes AS
Earth up vegetables that require it AS
Lift and dry onions, shallots and garlic LS

Herbs

Continue to remove dead stems from
herbaceous material AW
Continue to prepare ground when
conditions allow AW
Use cloches for protection or to promote
winter growth AW

Herbs

Finish removing last year's dead growth ES
Sow seed for annuals and perennials ES
Sow tender herbs ready for planting out
after frosts MS–LS
Plant out hardy herbs AS
Prune shrubby herbs ES
Plant out tender herbs after last frosts LS
Take basal cuttings ES–MS
Divide herbaceous herbs ES–MS

Herbs

Harvest herbs as required AS
Harvest herbs for storing before they flower ES–MS
Plant out tender herbs ES
Deadhead as necessary unless seed is required AS
Cut back herbaceous plant to stimulate
new growth AS

Fruit

Prune fruit bushes AW
Prune apple and pear trees AW
Heel in bare-rooted trees and bushes when
they arrive AW
Plant bushes and trees when conditions allow AW
Prevent birds stripping buds from fruit bushes AW–LW
Check stored fruit AW
Check supports and ties on supported
trees and bushes AW
Take hardwood cuttings EW

Fruit

Mulch bushes and trees with manure ES–MS
Finish winter pruning ES
Remove any winter-damaged branches ES
Finish planting bushes and trees ES
Hand-pollinate early fruit trees ES
Protect blossom from frosts AS
Prune plum trees LS
Thin gooseberries LS
Mulch strawberries with straw LS

Fruit

Pick early soft fruit ES–MS
Continue to pick soft fruit MS–LS
Pick cherries and early tree fruits MS
Net soft fruit against birds AS
Tie in new growth on cane fruit AS
Summer prune tree fruit AS
Thin tree fruit if necessary ES–MS
Remove spent raspberry canes and tie in
new growth LS
Remove foliage and mulch from spent strawberries LS
Pot up or transplant strawberry runners LS
Tip-layer briar fruit LS

Autumn

AA *all autumn* **EA** *early autumn* **MA** *mid-autumn*
LA *late autumn*

General
Continue weeding **AA**
Compost all waste vegetation **AA**
Water if necessary **EA**
Start autumn digging on heavy soils **MA–LA**
Clean and oil tools before putting away for winter **LA**

Vegetables
Lift and store potatoes **EA–MA**
Lift and store root crops in cold areas **LA**
Remove and compost finished crops **AA**
Plant garlic **LA**
Plant spring cabbage **EA**
Sow broad (fava) beans **LA**
Sow salad crops under glass **EA**
Protect globe artichokes, celeriac (celery root) and
celery with straw in cold areas **LA**
Protect brassicas from birds **AA**
Check stored vegetables **LA**

Herbs
Harvest seed as it ripens **AA**
Tidy away dead material as necessary **AA**
Protect tender herbs **MA–LA**
Plant perennial and shrubby herbs **AA**
Move container herbs under protection **MA–LA**
Divide herbaceous herbs **EA**

Fruit
Pick tree fruit as it ripens **AA**
Store apples and pears **AA**
Pick late crops of strawberries and raspberries **AA**
Plant new strawberry beds **EA, MA**
Remove old fruiting canes from briar fruit and
tie in the new **MA**
Finish removing old raspberry canes and tying
in the new **EA**
Take hardwood cuttings **LA**
Plant new fruit trees and bushes **MA–LA**
Check stored fruit **LA**
Check all supports and ties **EA–MA**

WINTER **It is advisable to protect permanent plants, such as globe artichokes, from winter cold and frost. A straw-filled box is a good source of insulation.**

SPRING **Leeks can be harvested between early autumn and late spring by simply digging them out with a fork. Autumn varieties are not as hardy and should be harvested before midwinter.**

SUMMER **Harvest globe artichokes, in summer, from the second year onwards. Take off the flower-heads before they open and while they are still green, cutting 2.5cm/1in below the head with a sharp knife or secateurs (pruners).**

AUTUMN **Potatoes can be harvested from early summer to autumn, depending on whether they are first earlies, second earlies or maincrop potatoes.**

INDEX

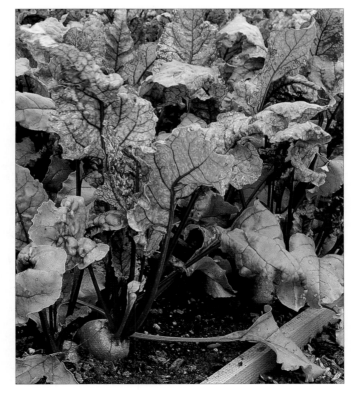

ACKNOWLEDGEMENTS

The publishers would like to thank the following for their permission to photograph their plants and gardens for this book:

Hilary and Richard Bird; the RHS Garden, Wisley; The Priest Huse, West Hoathley, Sussex

KEY
l = left; r = right; t = top; b = bottom; c = centre

The publishers would also like to thank the following picture agencies for allowing their pictures to be reproduced in this book:

The Garden Picture Library:
pages 13t (Alec Scaresbrook); 15t (Lamontagne); 28t (John Glover); 28b (Brian Carter); 29t (Mayer/Le Scanff); 29b (Howard Rice); 35t (Gil Hanly); 38l (Chris Burrows); 38r (Chris Burrows); 40br (Christopher Fairweather); 42l (Mayer/Le Scanff); 44t (David Askham); 45t (Mayer/Le Scanff); 53 (Ron Sutherland); 56b (Michael Viard); 65t (Lamontagne); 66 (Brian Carter); 67t (Lamontagne); 76b (Michael Howes); 79t (Lamontagne); 83t (Howard Rice); 83b (Lamontagne).

The Harry Smith Collection:
pages 14t; 36; 37l;40t; 57l; 57r; 61t and 77l.

GROWING FRUIT AND VEGETABLES